MASTERING

ENGLISH LANGUAGE

MACMILLAN MASTER SERIES

Basic Management
Biology
Chemistry
Commerce
Computer Programming
Computers
Data Processing
Economics
Electronics
English Language
French
German
Italian
Marketing
Mathematics
Modern World History
Office Practice
Physics
Principles of Accounts
Sociology
Spanish
Statistics
Study Skills

OTHER BOOKS BY THE SAME AUTHOR INCLUDE

Comprehension Practice
English Study and Composition
Modern Précis Practice
A Comprehensive English Course
The Criticism of Poetry
The Criticism of Prose

MASTERING
ENGLISH LANGUAGE

S. H. BURTON

First published 1982 by
THE MACMILLAN PRESS LTD
Companies and representatives
throughout the world

ISBN 0 333 31290 2 (hard cover)
        0 333 31032 2 (paper cover – home edition)
        0 333 31062 4 (paper cover – export edition)

Typeset by
REPRODUCTION DRAWINGS LTD
Sutton, Surrey

Printed and bound in Hong Kong

This book is also available under the title
Basic English Language
published by Macmillan Education.

CONTENTS

CONTENTS

PREFACE

All the English Language work tested in basic school and college examinations is covered in this book. It has been my aim to combine thoroughness of detail with practical applications of the skills required. I believe that the student who uses the book methodically will grow in confidence and competence as he prepares himself for the composition, practical writing, comprehension tests, and summary required of him in the examination. The step-by-step teaching comes to grips with the difficulties commonly experienced at this stage of English Language studies.

S H Burton

ACKNOWLEDGEMENTS

The author and publishers wish to thank the following, who have kindly given permission for the use of copyright material:

William Collins Sons & Co. Ltd, for an extract from *Sundry Creditors* by Nigel Balchin (1953); Constable & Co. Ltd, for an extract from *Journey Through Britain* by John Hillaby; Penguin Books Ltd, for extract from *Access for All* by K. H. Schaeffer and Elliott Sclar (1975), also *Man and Environment* by Robert Arvill; Weidenfeld (Publishers) Ltd, for an extract from *The Millstone* by Margaret Drabble.

CHAPTER 1

COMPOSITION

1.1 DIFFERENT KINDS OF COMPOSITION

(a) Composition in the examination

All examining boards require candidates in English Language to write a composition, and most of them allot more marks to this than to any other question. The composition is sometimes called an 'essay', sometimes 'continuous writing'. Whatever name is given to it, the question requires the candidate to write in 50 to 60 minutes an answer consisting of two or three pages of prose.

Most examining boards include another kind of composition question. This is given various names, of which the most common are 'practical writing' and 'factual writing'. This kind of writing is tested in a separate question – sometimes in a separate paper – but, like the 'essay' question, it is primarily a test of the candidate's ability to write good English prose.

Those two kinds of writing are discussed in the first two chapters of this book, and the different demands that they make on the candidate are thoroughly explored.

Do not forget that, in your answers to both kinds of question, the examiners are looking for:

- correctness of grammar, punctuation, and spelling;
- well-made and varied sentences;
- a well-planned piece of writing, tidily set out.

Lively and imaginative work will always be given extra marks, but it is the candidate's ability to write well-organised, clear, and accurate English that is the examiners' first concern.

(b) Imaginative writing / Practical writing

Bearing in mind that the qualities of good English (as described in the paragraph you have just read) are required in all writing, it is useful to consider composition under the two headings:

- 'Imaginative' (or 'Creative');
- 'Practical' (or 'Factual').

Those terms describe the two different kinds of writing that the examiners are looking for. They also point to the different mental activities that the different kinds of question demand.

Here, for example, are two examination questions that illustrate the two different kinds of writing expected of candidates:

1 Write a story entitled 'A Narrow Escape'.
2 Write a description of how to mend a puncture in a bicycle tyre. Your description should be written for the benefit of a reader who has never performed that operation.

Clearly, Question 1 is a subject for imaginative or creative composition, while Question 2 is a subject for practical or factual composition.

In answering Question 1 the candidate must imagine or create the material that he uses in the composition. In answering Question 2 the candidate must draw on his knowledge of the facts and his practical experience of how the thing is done.

Another difference between the two is the degree of control that each question imposes on the candidate. Question 1 leaves the writer with a lot of freedom to make his own personal response to the subject. Question 2 defines the subject clearly and strictly and, by the way in which the instructions are worded, exercises considerable control over the writer's response to the subject that he has been given.

The examining boards emphasise the difference between imaginative or creative writing on the one hand and practical or factual writing on the other. Here are some quotations from the syllabus regulations of various boards that illustrate the different qualities that are tested by the two kinds of writing.

1 Candidates will be asked to choose two subjects for composition, one from Section A, one from Section B. Those in Section A will be factual . . . with the subjects clearly delimited, and will call for a controlled response. In Section B the subjects will normally be . . . imaginative, allowing a much freer response.

2 Candidates will be required to write (a) a composition chosen from a number of subjects . . . (b) an exercise designed to test ability in the more practical aspects of expression.

3 Section A will test the candidate's ability to communicate what is required in a practical situation indicated in given material. Section B will test the candidate's ability to express himself at greater length . . . and will provide opportunity for imaginative writing.

The essential difference between the two kinds of composition that the examiners demand can be summed up like this:

Imaginative composition	*Practical composition*
Free treatment of	Controlled treatment
created material	of factual material

It would, however, be a mistake to think that an imaginative composition does not demand careful planning or that a practical composition does not demand imagination. In this chapter and in the next we discuss the planning and the imaginative demands of both 'free' and 'controlled' writing of the kind that examination candidates are required to undertake in composition questions.

Test 1
Answers on page 169.
Which of the following composition subjects are imaginative (or creative) and which are practical (or factual)? Mark each with I or P to indicate your answer.

1 Describe a ballpoint pen. Assume that the reader of your description is not familiar with this kind of writing instrument. Do not exceed 250 words.

2 Describe the sounds of early morning either in the country or in the town. Your composition should be about 500 words in length.

3 Write, in not more than 250 words, instructions to enable a stranger to find his way from your college or your school to your home.

4 Give an account of a television programme that you have enjoyed and describe those qualities of the programme that you found especially pleasing. You are allowed up to 400 words.

5 In not more than 500 words write a composition entitled 'The Treasure of the Sea'.

Test 2
When you have thought out your answers to the questions in this test turn to page 169 where you will find some ideas that may help you to take your own answers a little further. Study these composition subjects and then answer the questions.

(i) Write a story entitled 'A Narrow Escape'.
(ii) Write a description of how to mend a puncture in a bicycle tyre.

Your description should be written for the benefit of a reader who has never performed that operation.

Questions

1 Suppose that you are a candidate in the examination room and you are considering the best ways of writing those two compositions. You realise that an imaginative composition is expected as an answer to the first question. Which seem to you to be the 'key words' in the instructions? ('Key words' are the words that tell you what the examiner is looking for. They contain the clues that enable you to decide what you must do to satisfy the requirements of the question.)

2 Having decided on the key words in Question (i) jot down notes of ideas that would be useful if you were making a detailed plan for your composition. (We shall be discussing composition plans later in this chapter.)

3 Which are the key words in Question (ii)?

4 Which of those key words in Question (ii) tell you that you must use your imagination when writing your answer even though this is a practical composition?

1.2 PLANNING YOUR TIME IN THE COMPOSITION QUESTION

Many examining boards allow one hour for the composition question. Some allow 50 minutes. You must find out how much time your own board allows and then practise writing compositions within the specified time limit.

When an hour is allowed a composition of from two to three sides of examination paper is expected. When 50 minutes is allowed a slightly shorter composition is looked for, but it is inadvisable to write much less than two sides.

You will find it helpful to think in terms of a composition consisting of five or six paragraphs. You can then keep this useful structure in mind as you plan your composition:

Introduction: Paragraph 1
Body of composition: Paragraphs 2, 3, 4 (and 5)
Conclusion: Paragraph 5 (or 6)

Do not aim to spend all your time in writing the composition. To do so would be to invite failure. There are other stages in the production of a good answer that are as vital to success as the actual writing. These stages are selection, planning, and revision.

The reasons for spending time on selection, planning, and revision lie in the syllabus requirements for success in the composition question. The various boards word those requirements differently, but the sense of them all is the same:

- plan your composition carefully, so that it has unity;
- paragraph clearly, so that your material is presented in a logical sequence;
- write in a style appropriate to your subject;
- be accurate in punctuation, spelling, and grammar;
- remember that marks are given for quality, not quantity – provided that you write a composition of the minimum length, as stipulated.

Each of those requirements is discussed in later sections of this chapter and in later chapters of this book.

For the moment we will look at the effect of those requirements on the way in which the candidate must divide up his time in the composition question.

When answering a question for which one hour is allowed the time allocation should be of this order:

- reading through the instructions at the head of the paper and making sure that you know exactly what you have to do – one or two minutes;
- reading through all the questions and making your choice – not more than five minutes;
- finding your material, selecting your 'angle of attack', planning your composition – not less than ten minutes;
- writing your composition – about 40 minutes;
- reading through your composition and correcting careless slips – not more than five minutes.

If your board allows less than one hour for the composition question it is the writing time that should be reduced, since in that case a shorter composition will be expected. The other stages described above are as important for success in a 50-minute question as in a 60-minute question *and they must not be skimped*.

Time allocations and planning in the practical writing question are discussed in Chapter 2.

1.3 IMAGINATIVE OR CREATIVE COMPOSITIONS

(a) The personal element in imaginative writing

You may have found the answer to Question 4 in Test 1 (Section 1.1) surprising. The instruction 'Give an account of a television programme' seems to suggest that a factual composition is expected. If a witness of a road accident were asked to give an account of what he saw a factual answer would certainly be expected. The question, however, introduced a personal element. The full instructions were: 'Give an account of a television programme *that· you have enjoyed* and describe those qualities *that you found especially pleasing.'* The words in italics show you that the material for the composition is to be found in a personal experience.

Consider these instructions:

1 Give an account of how a television programme is produced.
2 Give an account of how a television programme is transmitted.
3 Give an account of a television programme that you have enjoyed.

You can see that 3 introduces a personal element that is not present in 1 and 2, both of which require factual, *objective* treatment. You would need to know a lot of technical facts to write on those subjects, and *you would be expected to confine your answer to those facts*.

When writing about 3, on the other hand, a personal approach is required. You would not be able to carry out the instructions without stating what it was that *you* enjoyed and describing the various ways in which the programme had given *you* pleasure: the excitement of the plot, or the quality of the acting, or the interest of the subject, or the delight of the humour - and so on, according to the kind of programme that *you* had chosen to describe and *your own reactions* to it.

In other words, 3 requires a mainly *subjective* treatment, whereas 1 and 2 require *objective* treatment. That contrast is fundamental to the distinction between imaginative or creative composition on the one hand and practical or factual writing on the other. The imaginative composition always demands that the writer *puts something of himself* into his writing.

(b) Different kinds of imaginative composition

Examination syllabuses refer to different kinds of imaginative compositions. Here are some examples: 'The subjects will normally be narrative, descriptive, or discursive.' 'The subjects may be descriptive, narrative, or controversial.' 'There will be opportunities to write a narrative, descriptive, discursive, or argumentative composition.' 'Dramatic, impressionistic, narrative, and discursive subjects will be included.'

Analysis of all the syllabuses and of past papers shows that the subjects set for composition may be classified under these headings:

1 Narrative
2 Descriptive
3 Discursive or argumentative or controversial
4 Dramatic or conversational
5 Impressionistic

The alternative names in common use are given in 3 and 4, above.

The requirements of each kind of imaginative composition are discussed, each in a separate section of this chapter. Before that, however, we will study a typical English Language Composition Paper.

English Language

Ordinary Level

COMPOSITION

Time: one hour
Write on one of the following subjects. Pay careful attention to punctuation, spelling, grammar, and handwriting.
1 Write a story entitled 'A Narrow Escape'.
2 Describe the sounds of early morning, either in the country or in the town.
3 Describe a visit that relatives or friends have paid to your home.
4 What are the advantages and disadvantages of the motor-car?
5 Magic.
6 An employer and one of his employees have had a disagreement. Outline the circumstances. Then write a conversation between the two in which they settle their differences.
7 What do the following lines suggest to you?

> And hushed they were, no noise of words
> In those bright cities ever rang;
> Only their thoughts, like golden birds,
> About their chambers thrilled and sang.

8 Write a composition about the ideas that this photograph brings to your mind.

(Candidates are supplied with a photograph – which may be a real life scene or a reproduction of a painting or a drawing – to enable them to answer Question 8.)

How do you decide which of those subjects to choose? You will recognise that different kinds of writing are called for by the different subjects set – narrative, descriptive, discursive, etc. – and in preparing yourself to take the examination you will probably have discovered that you are better at some kinds of writing than others. Even so, it would not be wise to choose, say, the discursive subject (4) just because you have generally gained good marks for discursive writing. Consider all the subjects carefully before you make your choice. It may be that you have no very clear ideas about this particular discursive subject and you may do better to choose, say, one of the descriptive subjects.

Remember, the prerequisite for a successful composition is to have a lively interest in your subject. You will do good work if you have personal experience of your chosen topic. Your imagination will then work on that experience to round it out into full and lively material which can be shaped into a well-planned piece of writing.

Test 3
Answers on page 169.
Identify the kind of writing – descriptive, discursive, etc. - that each subject in that examination paper calls for.

As your answers to Test 3 will have shown, some subjects can profitably be given a mixed treatment. The important thing is to think hard about each topic and to decide on your 'angle of attack' in the light of the subject-matter and the way in which the question is worded (see Section 1.4).

1.4 NARRATIVE COMPOSITIONS

(a) Having a story to tell – and telling it well
Everybody has the material for dozens of stories - life sees to that. True, but what a mess most people make of telling their stories! Everyday conversations afford abundant proof that few people are natural story-tellers. 'I should have explained that Tom's letter arrived after Jill saw Meg. That made all the difference.' 'Of course, you really have to know my uncle to see how funny that was.' 'No, wait a minute . . . I'm forgetting. It was in July, just *before* we went away.'

In the time that the examination allows, and in the space permitted, it is a difficult task to write a successful story. Even professional writers of fiction recognise that a short story is hard to write - and they are not tied down so firmly by time and length limitations. Nor do they have either a title or some other such rigid constraint laid upon them as the examination candidate does.

So, think hard before you choose a narrative composition in the examination. I am not saying that you should never attempt the story question. The examiners are not setting an impossible task, nor do they expect an impossibly high standard. They do not expect the candidate to reveal the talents of a professional. An interesting, well-planned story told in correct English will get a good mark. Just remember that a narrative composition is not an easy option.

(b) Finding the material

Obviously, the first requirement of a story composition is that it must interest the reader. This is true, of course, of the other kinds of composition. The candidate who bores the examiner is not making things easy for himself, whatever kind of composition he chooses; but a story is associated with leisure reading – with reading for pleasure. By choosing to write a story the candidate promises his reader an entertaining experience. The examiner will not be pleased if he is bored by the other kinds of composition, but he will not feel quite so disappointed – so let down – as by reading a boring story.

We saw in Section 1.3 that the essence of the imaginative composition is that the writer puts something of himself into his writing. This is particularly true of the narrative composition.

Consider the narrative question in the paper on page 7: 'Write a story entitled "A Narrow Escape".' It is the sort of title that seems so easy to tackle that many candidates rush at it, basing their stories on half-recalled newspaper reports of last-minute goals that were/were not scored, or vague memories of television spy/detective series full of close shaves. Such material results in poor quality 'formula writing', and the unfortunate examiner is condemned to an unvaried diet of stale, secondhand stuff.

An interesting story has originality; and originality does not depend on the frantic invention of far-fetched episodes and improbable details. Nor is it present in pale imitations of professionally written 'formula pieces'. Originality is achieved when the writer puts something of himself into his composition.

So, when you are considering 'A Narrow Escape' as a possible composition subject ask yourself, 'What personal experience can I put into this story?' That does not mean that all the details of the plot or the characters in your story must have a factual basis – power of invention is rightly valued by the reader. It *does* mean that the idea for your story should spring out of your *own* experience, not somebody else's. Your imagination should be working on material that means something to you. If not, your story cannot come alive.

Test 4

There are no right or wrong answers for this Test. I suggest that you work out some ideas, making notes, and then discuss them with another student who is working for the same examination.

1 Think of ways in which you might be able to use these real life happenings (some of which you will have experienced) as the basis for a story composition called 'A Narrow Escape'.

- you nearly miss a train or a bus
- the passmark in a test is 42 per cent; your mark is 43

- on the point of buying a present for a relative you discover by chance that he/she has a strong dislike of that particular thing
- in conversation with a newly made acquaintance at a social gathering you have begun to reveal to him/her your disapproval of a third party also present when your acquaintance mentions that this person is a friend/relative – you have to do some quick talking to extricate yourself from an embarrassing situation
- you are being interviewed for a job and in the course of the interview you realise how little you like the prospect of working for the person who is interviewing you and who seems to be favourably impressed with you as a candidate

2 Sketch out the details of a situation that you have experienced (not one of those outlined in 1, above) that would provide the basis for a story called 'A Narrow Escape'.

(c) Stories need plots, people, and atmosphere
A lot of planning is needed to turn the raw material for a story into a successful narrative. The writer can start work on his plan when he is sure that his material

- interests him and, therefore, stands a chance of interesting his reader
- is rooted in his own experience (i.e. is firsthand and fresh, not secondhand and stale)
- is capable of being used for a story of the kind asked for.

The first step in planning is to work out a *plot* for the story. This need not be elaborate. The examiner does not expect the examination candidate to be a professional writer of stories. But any story – if it is to be a story – must have a 'story line'. It cannot be static. It must move towards a conclusion. The situation depicted at the beginning must change into a different situation as the story unfolds.

The need for progression in the narrative is particularly important in the writing of 'puzzle stories' of the kind so often set in examination. Typical instructions for the writing of such stories are: 'Write a story ending with this sentence, "She was thankful that she had not won that prize"' or 'Write a story ending with this sentence, "I never did discover the name of the girl on the bus."'

Unless you have a gift for clever plotting such puzzle stories present you with a difficult task. Even simpler 'story lines' (those suited to the kind of story called for in 'A Narrow Escape') need to be worked out with care and planned in detail before you start writing. It is no use discovering half-way through that the story is not going to work out. There is not time in the examination to scrap half your work and start again.

Everything that happens in the story must be a development carrying the narrative forward. At the end, the situation depicted at the beginning has been resolved into a new state of affairs, linked to but different from the starting-point.

You cannot hope to hold your reader's interest unless you provide him with a well-organised and credible story line.

The story teller must learn to pace himself, too. At times he moves his story swiftly towards its climax. At times his narrative lingers to set scenes or to build suspense. Action and description alternate. The beginning, the middle, and the end are carefully proportioned to give the story shape.

The story must be about *people*. It must contain 'characters', as they are usually called. The reader needs to recognise the people in the story as 'real' people. If he cannot do this he cannot get interested in them. He does not have to like them all. He may feel liking or disliking, admiration or contempt, friendship or enmity, etc., for any of them, but he must *feel something* about them. He must understand why they are as they are and why they do what they do.

To involve his reader with his characters the writer of the story must believe in his people and be interested in them. Then, he needs the technical skill to bring them to life. He has to describe what they feel and think as well as what they do. He has to give them motives for their conduct. He has to reveal their natures through their words as well as through their deeds. To do this involves the writing of credible dialogue as well as the ability to describe scenes and narrate events.

Finally, the story must have *atmosphere*. Stories do not happen in a vacuum peopled by shadows. There has to be a setting - places, houses, furniture, weather, cars, possessions. People have looks, voices, mannerisms; they laugh, cry, wear clothes, are old, young, thin, fat.

The blending of people, events and setting creates atmosphere; and the writer needs a vivid but controlled imagination to build up an atmosphere that makes an impact on the reader and draws him into the story.

To sum up. The writer of a successful story needs narrative skill, dramatic skill, descriptive skill. A tall order, you may think. It is - but some candidates possess the necessary talents and, by harnessing them through careful planning, succeed in writing good stories under examination conditions. Study and practice along the lines suggested in this book will enable you to discover whether you have the ability to write a good story and, therefore, whether you would be wise to choose the story question in the composition paper.

Test 5

Study these instructions for a narrative composition and then work through the questions that follow.

Write a story entitled 'A Mysterious Messenger'. Try to build up an atmosphere of suspense and fear.

Questions

1 On what kind of personal experience could this story be based? If you have had such an experience – or if somebody you know has – outline it.

2 The instructions lay stress on producing atmosphere, but you will need to put people into your story first. How many people are you putting in your story? Who are they? Be specific about them: ages, sex, relationships, voices, looks, etc.

3 What is your story line? Where and how does your story begin? Where and how does it end? How does it get to that end from that beginning? What changes are brought about as your story moves towards its resolution?

4 What ingredients are you using to create the stipulated atmosphere of suspense and fear? To keep your reader in suspense you must keep him guessing about what is going to happen next; and you must make him want to know what is going to happen next. How will you communicate fear? Is somebody's life in danger? The atmosphere is generated partly by events and partly by people, but narrative and characterisation must be reinforced by the use of descriptive detail. Your reader must be excited by the story, believe in the people, *and* be convinced by the descriptive details. Skilful use of sights, sounds, and smells, by appealing to his senses, can immerse your reader in the story that you are telling. So, what is your *setting* for your story? Is it a lonely house? – a deserted lane? – is it daytime or night time? These details you must settle. If you can stimulate your reader's imagination he will co-operate with you and be eager to share in the experience that you are offering.

Working through Test 5 should have given you insight into the opportunities and the difficulties of story composition. Do not close your mind to the possibility of choosing such a question in the examination. Much depends on the wording of the question. It may be suited to you because you can see at once how to use a personal experience as the basis of a story along the lines stipulated. The work that you are doing now will help you to make a good decision when you see the questions.

1.5 DESCRIPTIVE COMPOSITIONS

(a) Carrying out the instructions

Descriptive composition subjects look easy. Anybody can describe the familiar scenes or objects that the examination questions usually specify and – unlike the story composition – the descriptive subject does not face the writer with a narrative problem. There is no story to tell.

Even so, the candidate must gather, select, and arrange his material carefully. The best way to start is to ask yourself the question: 'What, exactly, am I being told to do?' By asking - *and answering* - that question before starting to write you can avoid the all-too-common mistake of writing off the point. It is because descriptive writing looks easy that candidates often produce irrelevant answers.

If we take Question 2 from the examination paper on page 7 we can work out the stages through which the planning of an answer should pass. Each step is an essential preliminary to writing a good descriptive composition. 'Describe the sounds of early morning, either in the country or in the town.'

Note first that the examiner asks for either country or town sounds - *not* both. That seems (indeed, it is) obvious, but many a candidate has failed because he ignored an examiner's 'either/or'.

Next, pick out the key words: *sounds, early morning*. The examiner is asking for a description of sounds - not sights, smells, or movements. So, do exactly what you are told to do, and concentrate on sounds.

Another restriction on the subject-matter that the writer can choose is laid down by 'early morning'. 'Morning' is easy: it lasts up to twelve noon. But 'early' involves the writer in making decisions. What is 'early morning', and how long does it last?

You may decide to write about the period between first light and breakfast time. Or you could decide to interpret 'early morning' as a very restricted period - the first moments of consciousness, perhaps.

There is no 'right' or 'wrong' answer to the interpretation of 'early morning'. You are free to decide for yourself *within* the common-sense *limits* that the wording of the question stipulates.

Already, it is plain that gathering the material for a descriptive composition requires clear thought. The subject may look easy, but you must chew it over thoroughly before it is safe to start writing.

(b) Finding the material

Recall the statement on page 6. 'The imaginative composition always demands that the writer puts something of himself into his writing.' As you are working out exactly what the examiner is telling you to do you may be panicking because you feel that you have not got enough material for the composition. The remedy is to make your thinking *personal* not general: *avoid* an *abstract* approach. Personalise your thinking and ample material will flood into your mind.

Take this subject and try to open your mind to it. Allow memories of your own personal experience of early morning sounds to well up. Not just any early morning, but the sounds of one particular early morning. Those sounds will be real and clear in your memory, and there is every hope that they will be real and clear to the examiner as he reads your composition.

Relying on personal experience helps you to write about real things; and because they are coming out of *your* experience they will be fresh and original and, therefore, interesting. If you go about collecting your material in this way you have the best chance of doing what the examiner has asked you to do *and* you will be putting something of yourself into your writing.

Let us see how this method might work out in practice. The candidate whose progress we are going to follow lives in a town, so he chooses town sounds - the sounds that he knows. He has settled on the moments at and just after first waking as his interpretation of 'early morning'. He feels that by restricting himself to a brief period of time he can write a tighter and better-planned composition. He foresees the danger of producing a long list of successive sounds strung together in an uninspired fashion if he extends the time period. He wants to avoid a mere catalogue description: 'next . . . and then . . . and then . . . '. (Remember, there are no 'laws' about this choice. A different candidate might write successfully about an extended period of time. Each candidate must make the decision that suits him. The essential thing is to *think hard* about your material and how *you* can best carry out the instructions.)

Next, the candidate writes the title of his composition on his rough paper: 'The sounds of early morning in the town.' This acts as a guide as he collects his material.

Then, he jots down all the ideas that come into his head as he recalls the sounds that he hears in those first moments of consciousness. At this stage of planning his composition he does not worry about the order in which he is going to arrange the separate items. Nor does he worry about collecting more items than he can use. Selecting the material and arranging it are later stages of the planning process.

Here is his first rough list:

alarm clock's bell - footsteps downstairs - door bangs somewhere in house - front door opens and closes - letterbox snaps shut - whistling from garden path - footsteps on path - gate slams - clink of milk bottles - hum of electric motor - traffic noise - heavy vehicle stopping - conversation from street - labouring of heavy vehicle in low gear - somebody singing - voice calling my name - water running - intermittent hum of vacuum cleaner - time pips on radio - announcer's voice - father's voice from garden - stairs creaking - mother's voice from kitchen - bird song - thump on bedroom door - father's voice through door - music on radio - car starts up - gates open - gate bolt drags across tarmac - engine revs - dies away - mother's voice - chink of plates, cups, saucers – footsteps on stairs – bedroom door opens – dog barks – piercing whistle of kettle

(c) Selecting and arranging the material

(i) Getting an 'angle of attack'. Having collected his material the candidate starts to get it into shape. His rough list of items is 'raw material' that must be processed into a successful composition. Those rough jottings record the result of his concentrated recollection of personal experience. They form the basis for a good piece of writing, but they have been noted down in any order, just as they sprang to mind. Now, they must be ordered and shaped – given meaning – before writing can begin. Ordering and shaping cannot take place until the writer has decided upon his angle of attack.

He reads through his notes, asking himself from what angle he is going to write about his subject. How can this raw material be hammered into shape?

He *could* take the items in chronological order. That would be an obvious order to choose, but in the case of a descriptive, imaginative composition such as this it is not likely to be a successful order. As we shall see in Chapter 2 chronological order is often the best order in factual writing because it is the natural order. In imaginative writing, however, chronological order can result in the dull and mechanical 'catalogue composition' that our candidate is rightly anxious to avoid.

Thinking hard about his raw material, the writer sees a possible shape emerging. The sounds that he has listed are of two kinds: sounds originating inside the house; sounds originating outside the house.

Again, his list contains sounds that originate inside his bedroom and sounds that originate in other parts of the house.

An angle of attack now suggests itself:

- the awakening sleeper at the centre of the 'world' that his composition will depict;
- the house and its other occupants in a circle round him;
- the outside world in another circle round the household.

Such a way of looking at the raw material offers the possibility of constructing a firm shape for the composition. Given such a shape the composition has a good chance of making a vivid impact on its reader.

(ii) Giving the composition unity. By *unity* we mean 'oneness'. A composition has unity when it is complete in itself and when all its parts are combined into a harmonious whole. There are *no false starts* and *no loose ends*. A composition that has unity makes a satisfying impression of wholeness – of a *design* clearly thought out and competently carried through.

That is why our candidate tried to find an angle of attack as he contemplated his raw material. Once he had decided on an *angle* from which he could start *shaping* the raw material into a *design* he was well on his way to imposing *unity* on his composition.

The particular angle of attack chosen by our candidate is only one of the many possible angles that might be selected, just as the raw material for the composition is his own individual material – the result of *his* recollection of *his* personal experience. Another candidate would come up with different raw material offering a different angle of attack. Imaginative composition is a personal activity; but the *method* of going about it, as described here, can be followed successfully by everybody.

(d) Planning the composition

Now that our candidate has an angle of attack and sees how to achieve unity for his composition, he can arrange his raw material into a detailed plan. As he does so he may reject some of his material as being *irrelevant* to his angle of attack. The inclusion of such material would *dilute* the unity that he is trying to achieve. He may add to the material. Having worked out a successful angle of attack he may be stimulated to recall other early morning sounds that bear upon his treatment of the subject, bringing added vividness and a sharper meaning to his composition.

Because our candidate has thought hard about his raw material and has evolved an imaginative angle of attack, he is confident enough to work out a *paragraphic plan* of his composition. This is the best kind of plan. It ensures tight control over the material as the compositions is being written. Using the plan you see here, the candidate is unlikely to ramble away from the point. Everything included in the plan contributes to the *development* of the description and to the *unity* of the composition.

Plan

The Sounds of Early Morning in the Town

Introduction: alarm clock breaks silence – hideous din erupts – I strangle noise

Paragraph 2: I listen to house sounds spilling into my room – an upstairs door bangs – water running – descending footsteps on stairs – chink of cups and saucers from kitchen – piercing whistle of kettle – faint time pips on radio – announcer's voice – faint – cannot hear what he is saying

Paragraph 3: ascending footsteps on stairs – different ones this time – thump at bedroom door – my father's voice – stairs creak again – voices from kitchen – back door opens and shuts – garden gates open – scrape of gate bolt across tarmac

Paragraph 4: bird song in garden – 'rat-tat' at front door – letterbox snaps to – footsteps on front path – clink of milk bottles – whistling – whine of electric motor – traffic noises in street – rumble of heavy vehicle – brief silence – shouted conversation – 'thud-thud' of big engine – gears engage – lumbering din increases – decreases – car in drive below my window – pauses – revs again – dies away

Conclusion: tap at my door – my mother's voice – traffic noise from street increases – I switch on my radio – 'rah, rah, rah'! – world's din overwhelms my private silence – morning is here – I am part of it

Test 6

I suggest that you discuss the questions in this test with fellow students who are preparing themselves to take the composition paper. Think out answers of your own and make notes of them before your discussions take place.

1 At certain points in that composition plan the noises increase and then decrease. At other points silence follows noise, lasts briefly, then noise again invades the silence. Find examples of each of these and try to explain how they are related to the writer's angle of attack.

2 Examine the contents of each paragraph and try to explain the contribution that each paragraph makes to the writer's angle of attack as set out on page 15.

3 Although the writer includes a lot of different noises in his plan he does not dilute the unity of his composition. Examine one or two of the details that he includes and try to explain how they fit into the composition as a whole.

4 Make a list of some of the features in that plan that prove that it is based on personal experience. Then ask yourself whether you could use that plan as the basis for a composition of your own on that subject. If you feel that you would have to make changes in the plan before you could use it, say exactly what changes you would have to make and give your reasons for making them.

(e) Finding a theme – and sticking to it

The candidate whose work we have been following realised that he would bore his reader if he presented him with a mere list of the sounds that he heard early in the morning. So, having gathered his material by recalling personal experience, he looked for his angle of attack and then drew up a plan that gave his composition a shape.

It is so important to give a descriptive composition a firm shape that we must spend a little more time on that topic.

As I said earlier, the subjects set for descriptive compositions are usually so familiar that this kind of question seems easier than it is.

In many ways a descriptive composition offers a candidate his best chance of success. It does not require the narrative skills of the story composition. It does not require the logical argument of the discursive composition. It does not require the technical and dramatic skills of the conversational (or dramatic) composition. It does not require the imaginative response to a given stimulus of the impressionistic composition.

But a descriptive composition is not an easy option. It imposes disciplines of its own on the writer, the most important of which is this: to write a successful descriptive composition the candidate must find a theme – and stick to it.

Take this descriptive subject as an example: 'Describe the scene from a bridge.' There can be few candidates who have not stood on a bridge, so nobody who chose this question would be short of material. Indeed, most candidates would have so much material that they would hardly know what to do with it.

The writer on this subject is in danger of falling into one or the other of two traps. Either he tries to cram everything in and produces a mishmash of a composition – overflowing with detail and boring. Or he realises the need to be selective, but fails to establish a clear principle of selection by which he can guide his choice of material. Then, his paragraphs have weak connections – there is no thread, no theme, no unity.

If you were tackling that descriptive subject (the scene from a bridge) in the examination you would first draw on your own experience to provide the raw material. Then you would try to impose shape on the raw material. How is it to be done?

Well, you could use a particular interest of your own from which to derive a theme for your description. Are you, for example, interested in fishing, in nature study, in transport, in history, in geography, in rowing? From any one of those angles (and there are many other possibilities) you could derive a theme for your description. Once you had your theme you could draw up your plan to ensure that each paragraph was linked with the others and that every single detail of your description added something to the total effect. Remember: 'no false starts and no loose ends'.

Or you could draw on your personal experience to impose a different kind of theme on your description. You might recall a particular occasion on which you stood on a bridge and gazed at the scene. A day, perhaps, when some happy, or sad, or exciting event took place, and the scene reflected the emotions in your mind. This would be a much more subjective approach to the subject than the one just suggested, but it would be entirely acceptable to the examiner and it could provide a tightly constructed and truly imaginative basis for your composition.

The possibilities for theme finding are endless. Each candidate is free to explore the themes that appeal to him as he gathers his own material.

If you practise descriptive composition writing along the lines described, you will learn to apply these two fundamental rules for success:

- find your raw material in your own personal experience;
- find a theme that gives shape to that material.

Test 7

The questions in this test should be discussed. By talking over your own answers and those of others you will improve your skill in gathering and planning the material for descriptive compositions.

(i) Here is a rough list of ideas for a descriptive composition entitled 'Camp Fires'. Study the list and try to shape the material by discovering a theme for a composition on this subject. (You may add material of your own if you find that it helps you to think of a theme.) Then draw up a paragraphic plan for your composition.

flames against dark night - safety precautions - not near buildings - best wood for fires - singing round fires - companionship at camp - joys of open-air life - how to get fire going in wet weather - cooking by camp fires - holiday spirit - appeals to sense of adventure - crackling of wood - damping down safely - smell of cooking - acrid smoke - where to find wood - don't break down fences - keep people back from fires - permission needed - Guy Fawkes celebrations - the fire that wouldn't burn - construction of a good fire - out of control - beacon fires in days gone by - celebrations and warnings - cave fires of ancient man - messages by fire - romance - practicality - fire is man's friend - a good servant - a dangerous master - industrial applications - steam

When discussing the plans it is important to notice what is left out as well as what is included. There is raw material in that list for several different themes. Since a good composition (one that has unity) will have *one* theme, it follows that material that does not bear on the chosen theme must be omitted.

(ii) Study this paragraphic plan for a composition entitled 'A Village Shop'. Then discuss the notes and answer the questions.

Plan

A Village Shop

Introduction: the only shop in the village - stocked everything, from food to films, from gum to garden seeds - shelves and floor stacked high - what I remember chiefly about shop is Mrs Jones, the proprietor

Paragraph 2: Mrs Jones - little, rosy-cheeked, busy woman - born in village - knew everybody - in many cases had known their parents before them - Mrs Jones was more than a shopkeeper - friend and adviser to whole village

Paragraph 3: Mrs Jones at work - small child told not to buy particular kind of sweets ('they upset you last time') - woman looking for birthday card ('That's the kind Mrs Robinson likes, dear') - pensioner being told how to apply for new pension book

Paragraph 4: she knew everybody's business - not a gossip or busybody -

people trusted Mrs Jones - talked to her - her gift of friendship
Paragraph 5: Mrs Jones knew everybody, yet few people knew much about Mrs Jones - only the doctor knew that she was ill (bad heart) - shock in village when shop not open one day - blinds drawn - door locked
Conclusion: she had made little money from shop - shop sold - turned into private house - village without shop - worse, village without Mrs Jones

Notes and Questions

1 That plan concentrates on the owner of the shop, not on the shop itself. The composition could have been planned from a different angle of attack. The Introduction suggests what that angle might have been. What is the angle suggested (but not adopted) there?

2 What angle of attack would you choose if you were writing a composition on this subject? Remember, the choice is yours. The angle chosen in the above plan is not necessarily better than the angle you might choose. The writer of the plan was anxious to avoid a 'catalogue composition', so he did not choose the obvious angle.

3 Notice that the writer of the plan included some descriptive detail in the introductory paragraph. Such 'scene setting' helps the reader to visualise (and to believe in) the shop. The use of descriptive detail about Mrs Jones in the second paragraph serves a similar purpose. Care has to be taken not to include more detail than is absolutely necessary, and the writer did not allow himself to be distracted from his chosen theme. He did not get carried away when describing the shop, the goods, or Mrs Jones's appearance. He used just enough detail about each to help the reader to 'see' them; but he had chosen as his theme Mrs Jones's influence on the life of the village, and he stuck to that theme. The composition writer must always guard against the temptation to switch themes as he writes.

4 Notice the careful paragraph links established in the plan. The end of each paragraph leads in to the beginning of the next.

5 Notice that the plan begins and ends with Mrs Jones. This 'rounding off' - like the paragraph links - is designed to establish and preserve the unity of the composition: 'no false starts and no loose ends'.

1.6 DISCURSIVE COMPOSITIONS

(a) What is meant by 'discursive'?
A discursive composition is one in which the writer arrives at a conclusion by reasoning. He considers in turn various aspects of his subject matter and then proceeds to make a statement of his own carefully-thought-out opinions about that subject.

The alternative names for discursive writing are 'argumentative writing' and 'controversial writing'. Those alternative names indicate what kind of subjects are set and what kind of treatment is expected.

Typical subjects for discursive compositions, as they are set in examination are:

The advantages and disadvantages of the motor-car.

The advantages and disadvantages of television.

State the arguments for and against fox-hunting and give your opinions on the subject.

Should boxing be banned in schools?

What is the case for compulsory school uniform, and what is your view of the matter?

Do you think that smoking should be banned by law?

(b) What are the examiners looking for?

The qualities expected in a discursive composition are these:

- a genuine interest in the subject under discussion and an adequate fund of information about that subject;
- the ability to see both sides of an argument and to present opposing views clearly, coolly and fairly;
- the ability to take account of objections while calmly and rationally coming down in favour of a considered opinion;
- the ability to move steadily through conflicting arguments and to present a clear conclusion at the end.

(c) Pitfalls to be avoided

(i) No conclusion. The 'advantages / disadvantages', 'for / against' type of question ('What are the advantages and disadvantages of the motor-car?') may lead you to forget that a conclusion is expected. You must present your own opinion of where the balance lies. You are expected to have a view and to express it.

(ii) A one-sided presentation. Do not be misled by the question type of subject – for example, 'Should boxing be banned in schools?' Whichever side you take you should consider the arguments *against* your point of view as well as those in its favour. Your opinion will carry more weight if you show an awareness of the arguments that are used against it.

(iii) An intemperate and prejudiced presentation of your view. Many of the topics set for discursive compositions are controversial. They arouse strong feelings. For example, 'State the arguments for and against fox-hunting and give your opinions on the subject.' The examiner does not want to read an angry denuciation of the views of those who differ from you. He is looking for a cool, reasoned examination of both sides of the question, followed by an equally cool and reasoned statement of your opinion based on the facts as you have presented them. You are expected to believe in the correctness of your opinions, but you are also expected to be a thinking person.

To sum up. Discursive (argumentative or controversial) compositions are:

- discursive, because they require the writer to reason his way to a conclusion;
- argumentative, because they require the writer to expound the arguments for and against and to make a reasoned choice between them;
- controversial, because they require the writer to keep cool and think clearly when dealing with a topic that stirs up strong feelings.

(d) Planning a discursive composition

The requirements for success in writing a discursive composition (see 'What are the examiners looking for?') point the way to an ideal structure for a piece of writing of this kind. That ideal structure is shaped like this: 1 Introduction; 2 Body of composition; 3 Conclusion.

Introduction: Brief lead-in to subject, stating its importance and topicality – perhaps also referring to its long history.

Body of composition: Paragraphs 2, 3, 4 (and 5), each dealing with one main aspect of the subject and presenting the arguments for and against.

Conclusion: Paragraph 5 (or 6) in which the writer gives his considered opinion, based on his cool, rational appraisal of the arguments as set out in the body of the composition.

If we apply that structure to one of the discursive topics listed on page 21 we arrive at a paragraphic plan such as this.

Plan

The advantages and disadvantages of the motor-car

Introduction: After first prejudices against motor-car (speed, noise, frightening animals and people, man with red flag walking in front, etc.) had been overcome its clear advantages for individual owner (personal convenience, flexibility of transport, pleasures of driving, etc.) seemed to outweigh any disadvantages. Only in comparatively recent years have its good qualities and effects been seriously questioned.

Paragraph 2: Aspect 1 – Individual choices and pleasures increased by ownership of cars.

For: Makes for individual freedom and happiness; creates abundant business and recreational opportunities.

Against: Has had serious effects on provision of public transport – bus and railway routes restricted – rural areas hard hit – traffic congestion in towns.

Paragraph 3: *Aspect 2* - Environmental and health effects.

For: Opportunities afforded for holidays away from crowds - weekend and evening recreational trips.

Against: Overcrowding in 'beauty spots' - pollution by noise and fumes - crowded roads lead to accidents - road deaths and injuries.
Paragraph 4: *Aspect 3* - Use of a finite fuel.

For: In fact, only small proportion of oil consumed in industrial societies is consumed by private motorists - domestic heating and industrial uses consume much more - cars of immediate future will use much less oil than present models.

Against: Oil is so valuable a resource that none should be consumed for private purposes of motorists - if cars were not available public would insist on politicians solving public transport problem. Absence of cars would solve (a) traffic congestion problem, (b) health hazard, (c) invasion of countryside by fleets of cars. Resources now put into manufacturing, maintaining, and fuelling private cars could be put into public systems for the good of all.

Conclusion: Little doubt that a law banning manufacture and ownership of cars for private use would be a serious blow to individual freedom. However, it seems likely that rising cost of cars and their fuel will solve the problem by making cars too expensive for all but very rich. Consequent improvement of public transport and reduction of accidents, health hazards, and environmental pressures will, in my opinion, outweigh disadvantages of disappearance of private motor-car.

That plan is set out in rather more detail than you would probably employ under examination conditions. Once your mind is engaged with a discursive topic you will find that your notes need be no more than 'signposts' to point your way *through* the arguments *to* the conclusion. It is, however, essential to make a plan that shows clearly the framework on which you will build your composition.

Study that paragraphic plan. Note that each paragraph in the body of the composition deals with *one* aspect of the subject, presenting the arguments for and against in turn. This makes for a clear *progression* towards the conclusion and - assuming that each aspect is important to an understanding of the subject - ensures thorough treatment of the subject.

Test 8
Question 1 in this test is intended for discussion and no answer is supplied. Questions 2, 3 and 4 have answers for which you will find my suggestions on page 169.

1 Are you satisfied with the writer's choice of aspects of that subject, as set out in the plan? Do they, in your opinion, enable him to discuss the

subject thoroughly? If you were writing on that subject would you choose different aspects? If so, name them and suggest in notes how you would deal with them. Do not try to deal with too many aspects. The length of time allowed will not permit you to deal with many more than are listed in the plan. The essential thing is to choose three or four vital aspects that go to the heart of the discursive topic.

2 Study the *order* in which the various aspects of the subject are presented in the paragraphic plan. What do you think the writer's reasons were for dealing with those aspects in that order?

3 I think there is a loose end to one of the writer's opinions in the conclusion of the composition. See if you can find one.

4 Try to summarise the writer's arguments and his conclusion in not more than two short sentences of your own. When you have done this compare your summary with mine (see page 170). If you find it difficult to make the summary the fault may lie with you or it may lie with the writer of the plan. The test of a good discursive composition is the *clarity of its arguments* and the *logic of its conclusion*. Those qualities should make it easy for a reader to summarise the writer's views briefly and clearly.

1.7 DRAMATIC OR CONVERSATIONAL COMPOSITIONS

(a) The kind of question set in the examination
The examination paper on page 7 contained a typical subject for dramatic or conversational composition: 'An employer and one of his employees have had a disagreement. Outline the circumstances. Then write a conversation between the two in which they settle their differences.'

(b) The demands that such a question makes
This is what a candidate must do to carry out those instructions:

- write a composition consisting of two parts - an outline of the circumstances in which the disagreement arose, followed by a conversation;
- create two characters - the employer and his employee;
- write a conversation between those two people that carries the initial situation forward and changes it - in other words, invent a story line that is unfolded through the spoken word (conversation) *not* through narration.

(c) The skills that such a composition requires
This kind of composition asks a lot of the writer.

(i) Descriptive and narrative skills are needed to put over the initial situation. If you choose such a question you will need to draw on personal experience as you present your outline of the circumstances in which the employer and the employee fell out. Those circumstances must be credible. Was it a disagreement about pay? Or about working conditions? Or about the clothes that the employee was wearing at work? There are many possibilities. The causes of the dispute must be realistic and interesting *and* they must be set out *briefly*, because the main part of the composition is the conversation.

(ii) Imaginative skills are needed to create the two people involved. Your reader must believe in them if he is to be interested in your composition. You do not have to create full-length characters as in a play, but you do have to bring them alive and make them recognisably different from each other. You have to convey the essence of your people swiftly. There is neither time nor space for static description. To do this does require some dramatic skill.

(iii) And dramatic skill is what is required when you write the conversation. Two people, by talking to each other, move the story line forward, finishing in a different situation from the one in which they started. This is the essence of the playwright's skill – which is why compositions of this kind are called 'dramatic'.

(iv) Technical skill is needed to represent the spoken word in writing. There are strict conventions of punctuation governing the use of direct speech (see Chapter 8). You have to get your punctuation right if your written conversation is to make sense. It is easy to slip up and spoil a good dialogue by failing to punctuate correctly.

(v) Appropriateness of style is required. Your two characters must speak in a way that gives an impression of 'real speech'. The speech characteristics of each must differ from the speech characteristics of the other. Your reader must be given a sense of the different personalities involved, otherwise he will lose interest in the changing situation as it moves towards the settlement of their dispute.

It is my belief that a dramatic or conversational composition is the hardest kind to write successfully. It presents severe challenges, which can be met only by those writers who have special skills and gifts.

You may well have those special gifts and skills, in which case, have a go - *provided that* the wording of the question is such that you can find your raw material in your own personal experience. Then you have a good chance of bringing the dialogue alive.

There are many different ways in which a conversational or dramatic question can be phrased. The question that we have been considering is a fair representative of the type, but the writer is sometimes instructed to move the situation towards conflict rather than towards reconciliation. Sometimes more than two people are specified in the instructions.

Whatever the particular stipulations of such a question, however, the

candidate is asked to depict *people* in a *changing situation* and to convey .
personal relationships – all by the use of *direct speech*.

1.8 IMPRESSIONISTIC COMPOSITIONS

(a) Two kinds of stimulus material
The stimulus material provided for this type of composition is designed to
'trigger off' the candidate's imagination. It usually takes one of two
different forms. The candidate is given either some lines of poetry or a
picture as a trigger for his imaginative response. Various instructions
accompany the poem or the picture.

(b) Picture material
The picture forms part of the examination 'pack' that the candidate finds
on his desk. It may be a photograph of an action scene (a 'still', perhaps,
of a dramatic moment in a television play or film, or a news photograph
from a newspaper or magazine). It may be a photographic reproduction of
an artist's drawing or painting, which may be comic or serious, making its
impact by realistic detail or by imaginative suggestion. The range of
possibilities is great.

The examiner may instruct the candidate to do one of several things:

- write a story based on the picture;
- write a description of what he sees in the picture;
- write an account of the thoughts and/or feelings that the picture
suggests to him.

Each of those instructions involves a different kind of writing, but –
whether the composition takes the form of a story, or of a description,
or of an account of the writer's thoughts and/or feelings – the answer
must be based on (must spring out of, we might say) the picture. The
writer has to use his eyes and study the picture closely before he begins
to write.

(c) A story based on a picture
A story based on a picture must have all the qualities of good narrative
discussed in Section 1.4. The advice given there need not be repeated
here, but there are some special points to note about this particular kind
of story-telling.

(i) If the picture is an action photograph imagine that you are one of
the people in the photograph or, perhaps, the person who took it. By
getting yourself into the scene in this imaginative way you bring the
photograph alive. You provide yourself with an angle from which to tell

your story. You involve yourself in the action. You get to know the people. You then have a good chance of holding your reader's interest.

(ii) Having 'identified' with one of the people in the picture try to work out credible and interesting relationships between your 'angle character' and other people in the picture.

(iii) Study facial expressions, gestures, clothes, ages, positions, as shown in the picture. Sharp observation of those details will help you to invent the action for your story. You have to 'interpret' the picture, decide *what* is happening and *why* it is happening. Then, you can decide what is going to happen in your story.

(d) A description based on a picture

A descriptive composition based on a picture must follow the guidelines set out in Section 1.5, but some additional advice is useful when you are given a visual starting-point.

(i) Study the picture carefully, paying close attention to the details. Look for your angle of attack in the relationship between the details and the overall effect of the picture.

(ii) Finding and maintaining an angle of attack is crucial for success in descriptive writing, as we already know. Given a picture stimulus the writer will find his angle of attack most readily *either* by narrowing the focus down from the picture as a whole to a specific detail *or* by concentrating first on a detail and then widening the focus to take in the whole of the picture.

(iii) Move progressively from your chosen starting-point to your foreseen end. Do not chop and change. Do not start with an overall view, move to a detail, move back to the whole, and back to a detail again. You will destroy the unity of your descriptive composition unless you consistently maintain the angle from which you have chosen to write.

(iv) The detail(s) with which you begin or end your description is carefully selected as having particular significance in relation to the picture as a whole. It is your imaginative capacity to see this significance and to establish interesting connections between your chosen detail(s) and the picture as a whole that makes or breaks your composition. The detail that fires your imagination may be anything: a woman's smile, the angle at which a cap is worn, a clenched first, a car parked on a double yellow line, a shabby suit, an open door, a shadow . . . Once you have perceived the part that it can play in a unified description, you are on your way to success.

(e) Thoughts and/or feelings suggested by a picture

If the examiner's instructions are worded like this, 'What thoughts (or feelings) does this picture suggest to you?' another kind of composition is wanted. Such a question gives the writer considerable freedom to use his imagination. Indeed, he can allow his thoughts/feelings to journey beyond the bounds of the picture. The picture is then simply a starting-point.

A word of caution is necessary, however. The subject-matter of the composition must be triggered by something in the picture. The writer is expected to start his imaginative journey from the visual stimulus provided.

A good plan for a picture composition of this kind would be:

Introduction: Brief description of the 'trigger detail' in the picture and of its immediate effect on the writer.
Body of composition: Three or four paragraphs describing the *linked* thoughts and/or feelings that the 'trigger' has 'set off' in the writer's mind. (N.B. - *linked* thoughts and/or feelings. It is essential to establish connections. Each paragraph must lead the reader on to the next.)
Conclusion: A final paragraph 'rounding off' the imaginative 'journey' on which the writer has taken his reader. A return to the 'trigger detail' that started the mental processes described in the composition.

(f) A composition based on a poem
When the stimulus material supplied is a poem (either a short complete poem or a short extract from a poem) the examiner asks the candidate to carry out writing tasks that are essentially the same as picture-based tasks. The candidate may be required to write a story based on the poem, or to write a descriptive composition based on the poem, or to give an account of the thoughts and/or feelings that the poem brings to his mind.

The verse set in the examination paper on page 7 is representative of the material used.

> And hushed they were, no noise of words
> In those bright cities ever rang;
> Only their thoughts, like golden birds,
> About their chambers thrilled and sang.

In that paper the examiner asked the candidate to describe what those lines suggested to him. He could equally well have asked the candidate to write a story based on the verse or to describe the scene that it depicts.

I shall now work on that subject just as I would if I were taking the examination. When you tackle the questions in Test 8, or if you choose a similar question in the examination, you will find it helpful to apply the method that I am now going to use.

(i) Just as a picture must be closely studied before you begin to plan your answer, so a poem must be attentively read. Only by careful reading and an imaginative response to the words can you open your mind to the stimulus. So, I read and I jot down the words that make the most vivid impressions on me: *hushed – noise of words – bright cities – rang – thoughts – golden birds – chambers – thrilled and sang.* (N.B. I am not claiming that those words are in any sense 'right'. I can only make an honest list of *my* reactions. Another reader might find other words more evocative. This is essentially a subjective response, but it is only by responding to the stimulus that an impressionistic composition can be written.)

(ii) I study my list. It is, after all, the raw material for my composition, so it merits close consideration. I find that I have noted down phrases (*noise of words – bright cities* etc.) as well as single words. I get the feeling that I am responding to some sort of pattern or design; that it is the *grouping* of words in the poem that is working on my imagination.

(iii) I follow up the suggestion. Why did I note down *thoughts*? On its own, it is not remarkable. But it is not on its own. It gets a 'charge' from words and phrases round it: 'noise of words . . . thoughts . . . like golden birds'. Further brooding over my jotted notes increases my sense of a mysterious pattern: *they* (whoever they are) live in *bright cities* – they do not speak, but their *thoughts* are like *golden birds* . . .

(iv) The 'trigger details' set my mind off on a journey. I see a brightly lit futuristic city made of gleaming metal. I see its inhabitants – not unhappy, though their chambers are cages – their singing thoughts are the songs of imprisoned birds. They are the inheritors of an unknown destiny, living in a gem-like light that plays upon them ceaselessly, and singing because they must.

I now have ample material for my impressionistic composition, and I make a plan for it along the lines suggested on page 128.

Of course, I have no means of knowing whether the poet intended his words to make those impressions on my mind. The four lines supplied in the examination paper do not permit me to check the 'accuracy' of my responses. In any case, 'accuracy' is irrelevant in this context. Nor did the examiner tell me to give an account of the poet's meaning. If he had wanted me to do that he would have supplied me with material from which it would be possible to make a logical deduction. No, the examiner asked me to describe what the lines of poetry *suggested* to *me*. He wanted me to write about the thoughts and/or feelings that the poetry brought into my mind. And that is what I have been preparing to do. I have been trying to respond imaginatively to a careful reading of the poetry. I have allowed the 'trigger words' to set my mind off on a journey and, by doing so, I have gathered the material for a plan on which to base my composition.

For practice
No answers are supplied. Discuss your work on the questions in this test with fellow students who have also prepared answers.

1 Find an action photograph in a newspaper or magazine and prepare a plan for a story composition based on it.

2 Try to use a family photograph as the stimulus material for this question. Borrow a photograph of a group of people of an older generation. Study it carefully and then write a five-paragraph plan for a composition in which you describe the thoughts and feelings that the photograph brings to your mind. It will be an illuminating experience if you discuss your composition plan with somebody who knows some of the people in the photograph, or perhaps you can discuss your plan with somebody who appears in the photograph.

3 Working along the lines suggested on pages 28-9 work out a plan for a composition as an answer to this question:

What do these lines of poetry bring to your mind?

> The eye can hardly pick them out
> From the cold shade they shelter in,
> Till wind distresses tail and mane;
> The one crops grass, and moves about
> - The other seeming to look on -
> And stands anonymous again.

4 Write one or more of the compositions for which you have prepared plans.

CHAPTER 2

PRACTICAL OR FACTUAL WRITING

2.1 WHAT IS EXPECTED OF THE CANDIDATE

(a) The examination regulations

As stated in Section 1.1 some examining boards include the practical (or factual) writing question in the composition paper; others make it part of a separate paper.

The practical writing exercise is usually given about half the marks awarded for the imaginative composition. The candidate is expected to write an answer of about one page in length, and about half the time allowed for the imaginative composition is allowed for the practical writing exercise.

(b) What the examiner is looking for

The practical writing exercise is designed to test the candidate's ability to:

- write correct English;
- make accurate use of the material supplied.

2.2 DIFFERENT KINDS OF PRACTICAL OR FACTUAL WRITING

The chief kinds of practical writing asked for are these: explanations; instructions; outlines; reports; letters. Here is a typical examination paper containing one of each of those kinds.

English Language
Ordinary Level

FACTUAL WRITING

Answer one of the following. Write about one page and spend about 30 minutes on the question.

1 Explain to a reader who does not play the game you choose one of the following: draughts; hockey, darts; rugby or association football.

2 Write instructions on how to mend a puncture in a bicycle tyre. Assume that your reader has not performed the operation, though he owns a bicycle. Give your answer a heading.

3 You and several friends have thought up a plan for raising money for an organisation or enterprise in which you are interested (e.g. raising funds for a new scout hut or collecting to buy a minibus for your school). You need the approval and support of adults in authority (e.g. your scoutmaster or headteacher) before you can implement your scheme. Write an outline of your proposals for them to study. Provide a suitable heading.

4 A distinguished visitor has spoken at a meeting of an organisation (e.g. a school philatelic society or a youth club orchestra) of which you are secretary. Write a report of the meeting suitable for publication in your local newspaper, remembering to provide your report with a suitable heading.

5 Your parents have told you that you can invite a friend to accompany you on the family summer holiday. Write a letter to your friend's parents, conveying the invitation and expressing the hope that they will allow your friend to join you and your parents.

2.3 THE PROBLEM OF ORDER

(a) Clarity and economy of writing

Practical compositions of all kinds demand clarity and economy of writing. Practical or factual writing is writing that gets things done. It is writing that is performed to achieve a clear-cut and practical result. That is why it is sometimes called *transactional* writing. The successful performance of writing that gets things done depends upon the writer's ability to be clear and not to waste words.

Your writing is likely to get things done if it possesses clarity and economy; and it will be clear and economical if you present your material in a *logical* order.

(b) Parts, stages, and steps

Your material will be presented in a logical order if you apply this method when planning your answer:

- when describing an appliance, a piece of apparatus or equipment (a ballpoint pen, for example) divide your material into *parts* corresponding to the component parts of the object being described;
- when describing or outlining a transaction (applying for a driving licence, for example) divide your material into *stages* corresponding to the stages of the transaction;
- when describing a process or giving instructions (how to boil an egg, how to knit a garment, how to find the way from *A* to *B*, for example) divide your material into *steps* corresponding to the steps that must be taken to perform the task that you are describing.

The application of that method ensures that you think clearly as you plan your answer. It helps you to answer the two questions that you must always ask yourself: 'Where do I begin?' and 'Where do I end?'

There may be some overlap between parts, stages, and steps. A report of a speech (see Question 4 on page 32) may be arranged in parts and in stages. The contents of the speech are divided into parts. The sequence in which the speech was delivered is divided into stages. Such an arrangement ensures that the reporter includes all the important items in the speech and that he presents them in a clear order.

As an example of how the methods works here is a plan for a report of a speech made to members of the Ironfields Industrial Archaeological Society at its Annual General Meeting.

Headline: President Warns Society Against Complacency

Introduction: AGM held in Ironfields Assembly Rooms on 31 May 19 -. Keynote address given by President of Society, Professor J. Smith of Midshire University.

Body of report - paragraph 2: President welcomed members - referred briefly to success of last year's social activities - reminded members that Society's main function was conservation and exploration of local sites of archaeological importance.

Body of report - paragraph 3: Referred to loss of the Common Road site - building development had taken place there without adequate exploration and recording of Town Mill ruins - speaker felt that greater determination on Society's part could have delayed development until excavation had been completed.

Body of report - paragraph 4: Turned to development now threatening site of 18th-century warehouses in Castle Square - pressure must be exerted on Ironfields Council to delay development - volunteer labour would be required from members - contributions to Society's emergency fund - concerted and urgent effort called for - united drive could save unique site.

Conclusion: Vote of thanks moved by Mr C. Jones, a founder member - Society would not fail to respond to inspiration provided by keynote address.

Test 9
Answer on page 170.
That report covers the keynote address given by the Society's President. Why, then, did the reporter base the conclusion of his report on material from the vote of thanks?

2.4 LETTER-WRITING

Analysis of practical writing exercises set by the various examining boards shows that about half the questions require the candidate to write his answer in the form of a letter. It is very likely, then, that you will have an opportunity of tackling this type of practical writing exercise in the examination.

(a) Different kinds of letters

There are three main kinds: formal letters; informal letters; business letters. Although you will not be asked to write a business letter, in the strict sense of that term, you will almost certainly have to write a formal letter. A formal letter has some of the qualities of a business letter, so we shall look at business letters later in this section.

Many of the letters that we have to write can be described as 'business/formal' letters. They are letters to business firms written by private individuals. For example, we write letters to firms that have advertised their products in newspapers and magazines. The purpose of such letters is to order goods, or to request free samples, or to ask for further information. Or we may write to a firm to complain about delay in supplying goods, or to express dissatisfaction with goods that we have bought. Or we may write to a business firm replying to a letter that we have received from one of the firm's employees writing on the firm's behalf.

Another kind of formal letter involves correspondence with people who have an official position. We ourselves may be writing to them in an official capacity of our own or simply as private individuals.

For example, as secretary of a school debating society you might have to write to a town councillor inviting him or her to take part in a debate on some topic connected with local government. In those circumstances you would be writing to the councillor in his/her official capacity and you would be writing in your own official capacity.

Or, as a private individual, you might write to the secretary of your examining board enquiring how to obtain a copy of the board's regulations and copies of past examination papers.

In those cases the letters that you would write would be formal. Efficiency in the writing of formal letters depends on the writer's ability to be 'business-like' (we shall return to that quality) and to 'hit the right note' (achieve an appropriate style of writing).

Informal letters are letters to friends and relatives. Business-like qualities are not the first consideration in such letters, which are much more 'free and easy' than formal letters. Hitting the right note is the first consideration in informal letter-writing.

(b) The conventions of letter-writing

All letters - formal, informal, business - must obey certain conventions. These conventions serve certain useful purposes. They are not time-wasting, old-fashioned devices, clung to out of mere habit. They are used because they increase the efficiency of correspondence by providing essential information in a clear and universally observed manner. That is why you will be *penalised in the examination* if you *fail to observe the conventions.*

The conventions that must be observed are set out in the sections that follow.

(c) The writer's address

Unless you are using writing-paper on which the address is printed you must always write your address on the first sheet of your letter. The customary place for your address is at the top of the sheet and at the right-hand side. There is a choice of styles, as the following examples show, but some examining boards insist on Style 1. You *must* find out whether your board lays down a rule about this. If it does, then - of course - you must use Style 1 in the examination and in all your preparatory practice.

Style 1

51 Oldport Street,

Midford,

Midshire.

MD16 1OS

Style 2

```
                          51  Oldport Street

                          Midford

                          Midshire

                          MD16 10S
```

Notes on Style 1

    1 Each line of the address (except the postcode line) is indented – i.e. it begins nearer to the righthand edge of the sheet than the line above. It is customary to set each line back at an angle of 45 degrees.

    2 The postcode line is not indented. It begins at the same distance from the edge of the sheet as the county line.

    3 Each line of the address ends with a comma, except the county line (the last line before the postcode) which ends with a full stop. The postcode line is *not* punctuated at all.

    4 Some writers insert a comma after the house number (51, Oldport Street) but that is not obligatory. The line looks less cluttered if that internal comma is omitted.

Notes on Style 2

    1 There is no indentation. Each line of the address begins at the same distance from the righthand edge of the sheet.

    2 There is no punctuation. Those who favour Style 2 argue that there is no need to pepper an address with either end-of-line or internal punctuation. Each separate item of the address is written on a separate line, so why use end-of-line commas and a final full stop?

(d) Advice on the choice between Styles 1 and 2

The sole (and, of course, vital) purpose of writing your address on the first sheet of your letter is to enable your correspondent to reply. Style 2 gives him all the information that he needs. It provides that information in a less-cluttered (and, therefore, clearer and more attractive) manner than Style 1, as you can see when the two styles are set out side-by-side.

```
    51 Oldport Street          51, Oldport Street,

    Midford                        Midford,

    Midshire                        Midshire.

    MD16 10S                        MD16 10S
```

But - *repeat* - find out what your examining board demands, and *obey*. In any case, Style 1 is entirely 'correct', so if you like it better, use it.

(e) The date
Letters must always be dated. In formal correspondence it is frequently necessary to refer to an earlier letter and to identify it by its date: 'Thank you for your letter of 31 May. I have given much thought to your proposals for rearranging the programme but . . . '

Informal letters that are undated can inconvenience and sometimes infuriate their recipient: 'I'm going to stay with Jean the day after tomorrow, so let me know before I go if you want me to give her a message.' An undated letter containing such a statement causes confusion and worry.

It is thoughtless and inefficient not to date letters. That is why you will lose marks if you forget to date your letter in the examination.

The date is written immediately under the address like this:

```
                        51 Oldport Street,

                            Midford,

                             Midshire.

                             MD16 10S

                        21 June 1981
```

Notes
1 The form of date used there - 21 June 1981 - is the form that is nowadays favoured. No punctuation. No 'st' after 21. Similarly, there would be no 'rd' after 3 and no 'th' after 5, etc.

2 These date forms are also acceptable:

21st June, 1981.

June 21st, 1981

21/6/81

21.6.81

I do not think that any one of those is as clear as the preferred form used above. They are all fussier. I have set them out in order of preference.

Test 10
Answers on page 170.
What disadvantages can you see in the date forms set out in Note 2, above? Check your answers with mine. It is worth taking trouble to decide on the best form of date to use - then stick to it.

(f) The salutation

A letter is written to somebody and it must, therefore, begin by naming that person:

Dear Mr Jones,

    I am writing to ask you if you will . . .

Dear John,

    Have you made up your mind about...

This initial naming of the recipient of the letter is a sort of greeting and it is called *the salutation*. Every letter must begin with a salutation.

The correct salutation for all formal letters, for all business letters, and for most informal letters is *Dear* . . .

Very informal letters marked by a close friendship or loving relationship can, of course, have warmer salutations than *Dear* . . . Such salutations are not your concern for examination purposes.

You must observe all the conventions that regulate the placing and capitalising of the salutation.

51 Oldport Street

Midford

Midshire

MD16 10S

21 June 1981

Dear Mr Jones,

    When I wrote to you on 20 May I . . .

Notes

1 Capital D for *Dear*.

2 Salutation ends with a comma - *Dear Mr Jones,* (the absence of a full stop after *Mr* is exaplained in Chapter 8).

3 The salutation begins close to the lefthand edge of the sheet.

4 The first line of the letter itself is indented. (All subsequent paragraphs in the letter begin with an indented line.)

5 The first word of the first line of the letter begins with a capital letter.

There are *no* exceptions to any of those rules. Failure to observe those rules in the examination will cost you marks.

Test 11

Answer on page 170.

What mistakes are there in the following salutations?

1 Dear Mr White
    Can you please let me know . . .

2 Dear Mrs Robinson, I hope that . . .

3 Dear June
What are you going to do at half term?

4 dear Miss Green —
    The next committee meeting will be . . .

(g) The formal close

The writer of a letter 'signs off' at the end of the letter. The formula used in this signing off is called *the formal close*.

        Yours sincerely,

          J. White

        Yours faithfully,

          T. B. Robinson

```
                                    Yours,

                                    Jane

                                    Yours ever,

                                    Betty
```

Notes

1 The formal close is placed at the bottom of the letter and on the righthand side of the sheet.

2 *Yours* begins with a *capital* letter, but *sincerely* or *faithfully* or *ever* (or whatever word is used after *Yours*) begins with a *small* letter.

3 The formal close line ends with a comma.

4 There is no full stop after the writer's signature.

5 N.B. *spelling*: sincerely (*e* between *r* and *l*).
       faithfully (double *l*).

Test 12
Answers on page 170.
What mistakes are there in the following?

1 Yours Sincerely,

   J. White

2 Yours sincerly,

   J. White.

3 Yours sincerely

   J. White

4 Yours Faithfully,

   T. B. Robinson.

5 Yours faithfully

   T. B. Robinson

```
6   Yours Ever
    Betty.
```

(h) Signing the letter

Never write Mr or Mrs or Miss or Ms *before* your name. The rules are these:
Male writer signs Alan B. Jones – no Mr needed
  or A. B. Jones (Mr)
Female writer signs A. B. Jones (Mrs or Miss or Ms)
  or Ann B. Jones (Mrs or Miss or Ms)

(i) Matching up the salutation and the formal close

When the salutation *names* the recipient the writer of a formal letter must always close with *Yours sincerely*. When the salutation does *not* name the recipient the writer of the letter must always close with *Yours faithfully*. So, when the salutation is, for example,

```
Dear Mr Brown,
```

or

```
Dear Mrs Green,
```

or

```
Dear John,
```

the formal close must be

```
                          Yours sincerely,
```

and when the salutation is

```
Dear Sir,
```

or

```
Dear Madam,
```

or

```
Dear Sirs,
```

the formal close must be

```
                          Yours faithfully,
```

and there are no exceptions to that rule.

An alternative formal close for *Yours faithfully* is *Yours truly*, but that is less used now than *Yours faithfully*.

An *informal* letter may, as we have seen, be closed *Yours*, or *Yours ever*, or with whatever close the degree of warmth between writer and recipient make appropriate.

A letter written to the editor of a newspaper for publication in the correspondence columns of the paper usually begins with the salutation *Sir* and ends with the close *Yours faithfully*.

(j) Planning the letter

Like any other composition a letter must be clearly planned. The three-part structure recommended earlier makes a good basis for a clear, easy-to-read letter: introduction – body of letter – conclusion.

Because the conventions of letter-writing must be observed the full plan for a letter is:

Address

Date

Salutation

    Introduction

        Body of letter

      Conclusion

Formal close

Signature

Use that plan as a check list when you are practising.

As in other compositions, each paragraph in the letter must deal with one aspect of the subject. The paragraphs must be linked and must be arranged in a logical sequence.

(k) A formal letter to study

This letter illustrates the points discussed so far. Study it carefully and use it as a working model when you are practising letter-writing.

Westcross College of Art,

Bank Street,

Westcross,

Westshire.

WS8 1BS

2 November 1981

Dear Professor Hands,

I am arranging next term's programme of weekly meetings for the Discussion Society of this College and I have been instructed by the Committee to ask if you will very kindly agree to be our guest speaker at one of those meetings.

We meet in the College Library at 7.30 p.m. each Wednesday. I should be grateful if you could speak to us on one of the following dates: 21 or 28 January; 18 February; or any Wednesday in March.

Naturally, the choice of subject is yours, but many students here have been following your current research into the later work of John Constable. If you were willing to speak on that subject you would, I know, give great pleasure to all our members.

Yours sincerely,

Jane Brown (*Miss*)

Hon. Sec. Westcross College Discussion Society

(1) An informal letter to study

As we have said, an informal letter is more free and easy than a formal letter. Even so, the writer of an informal letter must take care to hit the right note. Many a friend and relative has been put out by receiving a letter written in an ill-judged style and, consequently, conveying an unfortunate tone. Again, when there are arrangements to make, the writer of an informal letter must be business-like – in other words, clear and crisp.

Study this informal letter. It provides guidance for your own practice.

26 Charlesworth Road,
Holly Bank,
Marden,
Northshire.
N H 11 16 HB

3 August 1981

Dear Jill,

I hope you're enjoying yourself, though I'm not writing this merely to wish you a happy holiday.

The point is this. You return on 15th, I think. Well, I've just seen in the local rag that the Festival Ballet is at the Hippodrome from 17 August to 23 August. Booking opens on Monday 10th.

Do you want me to get a seat for you? I'm hoping to book for myself for Wednesday 19th ('Giselle'). If you want me to book for you as well, let me know by return. The seats will go like hot cakes, so I must be at the Box Office when it opens on 10th.

I do, of course, hope that you are all having a splendid time — and better weather than here at home. Give my love to your parents, please.

Yours,
Mary

(m) A business letter to study

Although, as has been said, you will not have to write a business letter (in the strict sense of the term) in the examination, you often receive such letters and have to reply to them. Some of the features of business letters are also found in formal letters, and the crisp clarity of a *good* business letter is a quality that you should try to achieve in your own formal letter.

Tel 6785 - 46463   Date 10 October 1981

Your ref

Our ref JS/OS

Miss C. White

6 The Crescent

Tanshead

TH15 7CR

Dear Madam

Lambswool cardigan: model number SN 333

We thank you for your letter of 3 October, together with your remittance of £11.95.

We regret to inform you that stocks of model SN 333 in the colour that you ordered ('Dreamblue') were exhausted within a few days of our advertisement's appearance in the Daily Trumpet.

However, we have ample stocks of SN 333, in the size that you specified, in both 'Fieldgreen' and 'Sunset'. Perhaps one or the other of those shades would be an acceptable alternative to your original choice?

If neither colour is acceptable we will refund your money at once. Perhaps you will very kindly let us have your instructions.

Yours faithfully

J. Smith

Manager

Mail Order Department

Snugwear Limited

Notes

1 The letterhead is printed so that the typist need fill in merely the details that apply to this particular letter – e.g. the date and the reference.

2 The reference – JS/OS – consists of the initials of the sender of the letter and those of the typist. This is a common reference system for business letters.

3 Although Miss White's name is typed in above her address at the top of the letter the salutation used is the impersonal 'Dear Madam'. This is the correct form in a business letter concerned with buying and selling.

4 The letter begins with a heading – *Lambswool cardigan; model number SN 333* – so that its subject-matter is clearly announced for the benefit of both the sender and the recipient. Such a heading is a sensible device to assist in keeping a business letter short and to the point.

5 The sender introduces his letter with a reference to the letter from Miss White that initiated the correspondence. In this way, he 'tunes in' his reader, making it easy for her to comprehend the purpose of the letter. In that same introductory sentence he acknowledges that Miss White's order and money have been received. All this is crisp and business-like.

6 In the body of the letter the writer explains clearly what the difficulty is, suggests a way out, and offers a refund should the recipient not wish to accept the suggested solution.

7 He ends with a courteous request for Miss White's instructions.

8 The formal close is 'Yours faithfully,' since Miss White is not named in the salutation.

9 The letter is signed, and the writer's name and official position in the firm are typed in below his signature. This gives the recipient the assurance that her reply will be dealt with by the responsible person. It will not wander aimlessly round an impersonal organisation, hoping to be dealt with by somebody.

Altogether, a good business-like business letter. (Not all business letters succeed in being business-like!)

Two final comments about layout and style now follow, in case you are puzzled by features that seem to contradict advice given earlier about the conventions. Remember that, in business letters, printed letterheads and sophisticated typing facilities permit successful variations in the layout and style that, as a private individual, it is better for you to adopt.

(i) The 'no indentation and open punctuation' style was adopted for the addresses typed in the letter. Open punctuation was also used after the salutation and the formal close. Open punctuation was also used when the sender's identification was typed at the bottom of the letter.

(ii) The letter layout followed the 'fully blocked' pattern, now much favoured for business letters. In other words, each line begins close to the lefthand margin and the first line of each paragraph is not indented.

Dear Madam

<u>Lambswool cardigan. . .</u>

We thank you . . .

Yours faithfully.

Manager

etc.

You will be well-advised to use the more traditional layout as illustrated in Miss White's reply to that letter (see page 50). In her letter the first line of each paragraph is indented and the date and the formal close are placed towards the righthand margin of the sheet. It is difficult to make a fully blocked layout look clear and attractive when you are writing by hand on a plain sheet of paper.

(n) A reply to a business letter (see page 50)

Notes

1 Miss White uses progressive indentation and closed punctuation both for her own address and when writing out the name of the recipient and his identification. She also ends the salutation and the formal close with a comma.

2 She does not write out the firm's address in full, but she does identify the person to whom she is writing by his name and his position. This is a sensible precaution. In many firms all incoming mail is opened in a post room, and a letter identifying its addressee will get on to his desk more quickly than one that is simply addressed to the firm.

3 She sensibly repeats the heading that appeared on the firm's letter. This is good practice: both parties to the correspondence are 'tuned in' to the matter being dealt with. The heading makes for economy of words.

4 Although she knows the name of her correspondent she quite rightly uses the impersonal salutation 'Dear Sir'. This is a reply to a business letter about buying and selling. She does not know Mr Smith personally, and he does not know her. Nor is their correspondence likely to develop. 'Sir' and 'Madam' are correct.

5 She signs her letter with her initials and her surname, adding in brackets 'Miss'.

6 The Crescent,
Tanshead.
YH 15 7CR

12 October 1981

Mr J. Smith,
Manager, Mail Order Department,
Snugwear Limited.

Dear Sir,

Lambswool cardigan: model number
SN 333

Thank you for your letter of 10 October.
I am sorry to learn that you have sold out
your stocks of model SN 333 in 'Dreamblue'.

Neither of the other shades that you
have in stock appeals to me, so I shall be
obliged if you will refund my money.

Yours faithfully,
C. White (Miss)

(o) Addressing the envelope
The rules that apply to the writing of addresses in the letter apply also to the writing of the address on the envelope. Care must also be taken to place the address so that the cancellation of the stamp does not obliterate any item of the address. Place the address towards the lefthand edge of the envelope and nearer to the bottom than to the top, but leave generous margins.

When addressing a man, business firms often use *Esq* ('Esquire') instead of *Mr*. The practice is by no means universal, and it is decreasing both in business and in private correspondence.

When it is used two rules must be obeyed:

1 Never use Mr *and* Esq. One *or* the other.

2 Esq can be used *only* when the initials of the addressee are known: 'J. A. E. Brown, Esq'.

(p) Postcards
They are useful for brief messages, but they are not suitable for correspondence on matters involving any degree of privacy. Postcards are a very public form of correspondence.

A postcard message does not begin with a salutation nor does it end with a formal close. It is usually signed with the initials or the forename of the sender.

Business firms make use of postcards for 'proforma' communications: 'Date as postmark. We acknowledge your order dated _____. The goods will be despatched on _____ . Please inform us if not received within 14 days of despatch.'

Test 13
When you have written your answers to this test exchange them with fellow students and give each other the benefit of friendly (but firm) criticism.
Write a letter suited to one or more of the following situations.

1 As the secretary of a fund-raising effort write to a television or radio personality asking him/her to donate a small personal possession to be auctioned at a fête that you are organising.

2 In your capacity as secretary of a school or college society write to a member of your county or district council asking the councillor to speak at a meeting of your club.

3 You are interested in a tour which a friend has told you has been advertised by a local coach firm. Unfortunately, you have not seen the advertisement and your friend has lost his copy of the newspaper in which

it appeared. Your mother has said that you can go on the tour and that she would like to accompany you. However, she is too busy to make the arrangements and she tells you to write the necessary letter of enquiry. (Think hard about the details that you will need to discover from the coach firm before you can make firm plans to go.)

4 A friend of yours has moved away to live in another part of the country. You have written to him/her once, but have not received a reply. Some months after his/her departure you hear a rumour that his/her mother, though now recovering, has been seriously ill. You do not know any details. Write a suitable letter to your friend.

5 The offer detailed in this advertisement is of interest to you, as you have been trying without success to obtain some books locally. Write a suitable letter to the firm.

PAPERBACKS UNLIMITED
Book House 60 Chase Street Milltown MT4 4CS

Frustrated by difficulty in obtaining that book you specially want? Even 'the latest' paperback is often unobtainable from local bookshops. Send us a list of your wants. We invoice you when your order is ready for despatch. We charge 50p p. & p. on each parcel, regardless of the number of books enclosed. Please give full details: title, author, publisher.

CHAPTER 3

COMPREHENSION

All the examining boards require candidates in English Language to answer comprehension questions and to write summaries. The marks allotted (exceeded only by those allotted to composition) reflect the importance that the examiners attach to this work.

Some examining boards provide two separate passages, setting comprehension questions on one and requiring candidates to write a summary of the other. Most boards provide one passage and use it as the material for both comprehension and summary.

The two activities are closely connected. You cannot summarise material that you have not comprehended. So, although each is given a chapter to itself in this book, that does not suggest that they involve separate mental processes. By allowing ample space for each we have room for thorough discussion of the thinking, planning, and writing necessary for successful answers to comprehension questions and for accurate summary.

3.1 WHAT IS COMPREHENSION?

(a) The meaning of 'comprehend'

Comprehend is a verb meaning 'to grasp with the mind, take in'. Comprehension, then, is 'the act of grasping with the mind, taking in'.

Though it can be said (correctly) that *comprehesion* means 'understanding' it is safer to think of it in terms of the definition given above. You are more likely to work along the right lines if you remind yourself that the examiner is asking you questions to test whether you have *grasped* the passage *with your mind – taken it in*.

Comprehension is understanding in *depth*. It is a grasping, a taking in, of the material with which you are required to deal.

Not many candidates score high marks for comprehension. This generally poor performance is due to widespread failure to appreciate what is meant by 'comprehension', in the full meaning of that word. Too few candidates have learnt to read with the concentrated and directed attention that is essential.

(b) How to comprehend

Very careful reading of the set passage is the first requirement. By 'careful reading' we mean reading with purpose and reading with imagination.

Lazy-minded, superficial reading is no use. Anybody can skim over the surface of the set passage – and fail! You must read with entire concentration, determined to master the meaning of the passage in front of you – determined to grasp it with your mind.

You must also read it sympathetically, entering into its spirit and working *with* the author. That is what is meant by 'reading with imagination'.

3.2 METHOD IN COMPREHENSION

(a) The method of reading the passage

Warning. It is a great mistake to read the questions *before* you have read the passage right through in the way that I am about to describe. If you read the questions before you read the passage you will be distracted from your first task, which is to take in the *general meaning* of the passage *as a whole*.

1 Read the passage right through once, concentrating your attention on what seems to be its main theme. In other words, *get the gist of it*. As soon as you have completed this first reading make a note of the main drift of the contents, like this:

> Writer argues that pace of industrial development must be slowed to conserve world's resources of minerals and fuel.

A similar note encapsulating the theme of a descriptive passage might read:

> Description of exceptional severity of winter of 1962/63 and of its effects on one rural community.

2 Read the passage right through a second time, bearing in mind the main drift as discovered during your first reading. During this second reading, pay attention to the spirit of the passage, noticing the key words and phrases and opening your mind to their implicit meaning as well as their explicit sense. You are 'reading between the lines' now, entering into the author's intentions, and noticing not only *what* is said but also *how* it is said. Notice, too, how the passage is developed. Trace the stages through which the writer's subject-matter is unfolded. Attention paid now to the structure of the passage will yield dividends later.

When you have completed those two readings you are ready to study the examiner's questions.

(b) Reading the questions

Read through *all* the questions first. Do not begin to answer any before you have studied them all. Careful reading of all the questions throws light on each separate question. More marks are lost in comprehension through misunderstanding the meaning of the questions than through any other cause.

When you have read all the questions, read through the passage once more, bearing the questions in mind. If your first two readings have been thorough and imaginative, as described in Section 3.2 (a), the questions will begin to 'make sense' during this third reading. This is a vital stage in your work. It is now that you see the purpose behind the questions and understand what the examiner was getting at when he selected these particular questions for this particular passage.

(c) Answering the questions

Having completed the third reading, begin to answer the questions. Try to work methodically through them in the order in which they appear on the examination paper. If you find that you are bogged down by a question do not spend too long agonising over it. Leave space for your answer to it on your rough paper and come back to it when you have drafted your answers to the later questions. It often happens that a question that baffles you at your first attempt to answer it falls into perspective as you answer others. The answer 'emerges' while you are working on the questions that come more easily to you. But *do remember* to leave a space for the missing answer. You are then less likely to forget to come back to it.

Nowhere else in the examination is it more important to answer the questions set, *not those that you think have been set*: in other words, to follow exactly the instructions that you have been given. Nowhere else is it easier to fall into the trap of answering the wrong question, or of answering the right question in the wrong way. These dangers arise because, as will be shown in detail in Section 3.3, comprehension questions necessarily appear in a great variety of forms.

So, if you are asked for a sentence answer, give a sentence answer. If you are asked for a one-word answer, answer in one word. (N.B. Unless instructed otherwise, write your answers in complete sentences.) If you are asked to write down four reasons why a character in a narrative passage did something, write down four reasons – neither less nor more. If you write down three you will get marks only for three. If you write down five or six you are wasting your precious time. The examiner will read the first four reasons in your answer and ignore the rest. You get no marks for doing what you were not told to do.

When you have answered all the questions on your rough paper, read through the questions and your answers again, checking that you have obeyed all the instructions and correcting any careless slips of spelling or grammar that you may have made.

Check, too, that your answers are accurately numbered to correspond with the numbering of the questions. The nature of comprehension exercises often involves rather complicated numeration. A question may well be numbered '2a(i)', or something equally complicated. So take care that your answer to that question is also numbered '2a(i)'.

Finally, copy out your answers, neatly and clearly, on to the answer sheet provided. And still leave time for a last read-through. It is so easy to make slips when copying from rough paper into the final form; and it is such a waste of marks to spoil carefully polished and corrected work by careless copying.

3.3 THE PASSAGES AND THE QUESTIONS

(a) The kinds of passages set for comprehension

As you saw in Chapter 1, there are many different kinds of writing. The passages set for comprehension reflect that variety. The passage that you find in your examination paper may be an example of narrative, or descriptive, or discursive, or dramatic, or impressionistic writing. It may be humorous, serious, satirical, factual, subjective, objective . . . and so on.

That is why the advice given earlier about entering into the spirit of the passage is of such importance. By discovering the writer's intentions and then cooperating with him you are preparing yourself in the best possible way to answer the examiner's questions.

Again, you must make an effort to take a lively interest in the subject-matter. It may be that the passage is about a topic new to you, or about a topic in which, up to now, you have had no interest whatever. Well, now is the time to get interested! Read with an open mind and read with purposeful, concentrated attention. Your interest will soon be kindled if you follow that advice.

Do not panic if you find that you know nothing about the subject on which the passage is written. Previous knowledge of the subject is not required. Total ignorance of the writer's topic is no handicap at all, *provided that* you prove that you have the ability to learn from the passage. You prove that you have that ability by the way in which you answer the questions you are asked.

Remember: all the questions can be answered by a candidate of average intelligence and imagination who reads the passage and the questions carefully. All the *facts* that you need to answer the questions that test your powers of observation *are contained in the passage*. The other questions can be answered by allowing your intelligence and imagination to respond to the writer's words. See again Section 3.2 (a) (p. 54).

(b) The kinds of questions set

As has just been said, some questions test your *powers of observation* by asking you about the *contents* of the passage. Other questions test your ability to read with intelligence and imagination - in other words, your ability to *think* about the passage and make an *imaginative response* to it.

It is important to recognise the kind of question that you are being asked, because you then know what kind of an answer is expected.

Here is a useful classification to bear in mind as you practise for the comprehension questions.

1 Questions about the *subject-matter* - the *contents*, the *meaning* - of the passage. These questions ask you *what* the writer has said.

Examples

(i) Using the information given in the passage state how old *X* was at the time this incident took place.

(ii) List three ways in which *Y* considers that the intruders may have gained access to the warehouse.

(iii) Give one example of inadequate supervision as detailed by *Z*.

2 Questions about the *style* of the passage. These questions ask you *how* the passage is written. They ask you about the writer's use of language, particularly his use of imagery and figures of speech. They ask you about the writer's control over and variety in the use of sentences and paragraphs.

Examples

(i) Bring out the force of the metaphors in the following quotations from the passage, paying special attention to the italicised words: '. . . the oak stood *sentinel* at the park entrance . . .' (1. -); '. . . briars *writhed* round the dilapidated cottage . . .' (1. -).

(ii) What effect does the writer achieve by his use of short sentences at the end of paragraph 3?

(iii) Discuss the varied lengths of the four paragraphs in the passage and show how that variety is used by the writer to help him to convey his theme to his reader.

3 Questions about *vocabulary*. These questions ask you about the writer's use of words, especially his use of unusual or difficult words, or about his use of ordinary words in an unusual and surprising way. They direct your attention to his ability to use *appropriate* words - i.e to match his choice of words to his subject matter and to his purposes in writing. Vocabulary questions are, thus, concerned both with *what* is written and with *how* it is written. They ask you to explain points either of meaning

or of style; but since they concentrate on individual words or phrases they merit a separate entry in this classification of types of questions.

Examples

(i) Explain the meaning of the following words as they are used in the passage: engulfed (1. -); peaked (1. -); casket (1. -).

(ii) Express in your own words the meaning of '. . . an acute perception of frailty and an unscrupulous capacity to play upon his adversary's vulnerability . . .' (11. - - -).

(iii) Give one word meaning the same as each of the following as used in the passage: tendentious (1. -); partisan (1. -); disinterested (1. -).

N.B. When answering questions such as those in (iii), above, you must supply a synonym *with the same grammatical function* as the word that you are explaining. For example, 'partisan' could be used either as a noun or as an adjective. If it is used in the passage as a noun you must supply a noun equivalent. If it is used in the passage as an adjective you must supply an adjective equivalent. If you answer with a word that is a different part of speech (see Chapter 6) you are *not* supplying a word that 'means the same', and you will lose marks.

4 Questions that test your ability to make an *imaginative response* to the contents of the passage. Such questions feature largely when the passage is an extract from narrative or dramatic writing.

Examples

(i) Describe the tone of voice in which *X* makes his answer to *Y*'s challenge and say what this tells you about his attitude to the situation in which he finds himself.

(ii) In one sentence (not more than 30 words) describe *A*'s relationship with *B*.

(iii) What does this quotation from the passage tell you about *C*'s character and about his motives in taking the action described? '. . . in his favourite and highly profitable role of public benefactor . . .'.

5 Questions that test your ability to *think* about the contents of the passage, particularly about the writer's use of argument and example. Such questions are often set when the passage is an extract from discursive writing.

Examples

(i) Select two statements from the passage that indicate *A*'s opinion of *B*'s arguments.

(ii) What details in the passage show that X was not thorough in researching the market for his product?

(iii) State briefly (not more than 35 words) your opinion of the conclusion to which the writer comes in the end. Pay special attention to the example that he uses in the last paragraph to support his final argument.

3.4 FOR PRACTICE

Typical examination questions are discussed in this section. Answers are given in some cases. Other questions are followed by commentaries and you are left to find your own answers along the lines suggested. We begin with short extracts from examination papers, the better to illustrate and put into practice the advice given. Later in the section you will find full-length passages with a complete range of questions to give you experience of working under examination conditions.

1

The walking city was mankind's answer to these transport problems. People collocated to be together for activities they considered important and for which transportation was too slow and too cumbersome. In turn, they planned and arranged their cities around the general principle of avoiding cumbersome internal transportation, both in terms of the necessary number of trips and the length of these trips. Such marks of the modern city as one-way streets, limited-access roads, or land-consuming road interchanges would have been an anathema to the city planners of the pre-motorized era. Consciously or unconsciously, the planners and builders of the walking cities searched for circulation patterns that assured access for the most essential functions by traveling the least distance. At first glance, a medieval town with its crooked streets may seem an inefficient design. However, if we look more carefully, the crooked street patterns suggest a circle with radial spokes and circumferential routes. When the town is on or against a hill, the crookedness may result from squeezing as many dwellings into the hillside as possible with the least cutting and filling. To cut and fill, the joy of modern architects and contractors, requires extensive transportation. The earth must be moved hither and yon. This is a backbreaking task if the tools are limited to pick, shovel, wheelbarrow and animal-drawn carts.

K. H. Schaeffer and Elliot Sclar: *Access for All*

Commentary

1 The authors describe the principle behind the planning and construction of what they call 'walking cities'. The key sentence is: 'Consciously or

unconsciously . . . by traveling the least distance.' (See later for a note on the spelling *traveling*.)

2 The subject-matter is rather 'technical' and specialised. The language used reflects this, for some rather unusual and difficult words are employed: *collocated*; *anathema*; *pre-motorized era*; *circumferential*. However, the writers have tried to keep their vocabulary and style as plain and direct as the subject permits. They make use of some vigorous, 'everyday' expressions - *trips*; *crooked streets*; *backbreaking task* - and their sentences are short. Consequently, they get their meaning across swiftly and unambiguously. One or two linguistic 'signals' indicate that this is 'American English' not 'English English'; for example, they spell *traveling* with one *l*, and they use the expression *hither and yon* instead of *hither and thither*.

Typical questions and suggested answers

1 State in your own words the two factors that the planners of the walking city had in mind when they tried to avoid cumbersome internal transportation.

Answer They planned their internal routes to reduce both the frequency and the length of the journeys that the city dwellers had to make. (*Evidence for answer* See sentence 3: 'In turn . . . of these trips.')

2 Name two of the tools available to the city builders described in the passage.

Answer (i) pick; (ii) shovel. (Those two tools were chosen from the list of four named in the last sentence of the passage.)

3 Explain in your own words the meaning of 'cutting' and 'filling' as used in the passage.

Answer *Cutting* means 'excavating'. *Filling* means 'levelling'.

4 Why were cutting and filling avoided by the builders of the walking city?

Answer Cutting and filling necessitate earth moving, a most laborious process when only primitive tools are available. (*Evidence for answer* See the last three sentences of the passage.)

5 Why, do you think, do the authors describe the city as 'the walking city'?

Answer Because the main form of transport was by walking. All journeys had to be made on foot or in carts pulled by walking animals. Consequently, the city layout and its routes were planned to make walking as efficient as possible. Walking dominated all city planning and building.

6 In what period were walking cities built?

Answer Walking cities were built in the medieval period. (*Evidence for answer* The authors use the expression 'a medieval town' as a synonym for 'the walking city': '. . . a medieval town with its crooked streets . . .'.)

7 Give in your own words and as briefly as you can the meaning of

each of the following as used in the passage (i) collocated; (ii) an anathema; (iii) the pre-motorized era; (iv) circumferential routes.

Answer (i) joined up in one place; (ii) something to be shunned; (iii) the period before the invention of motor cars and lorries; (iv) lines of travel following the rim of a circle. (*Note on answer* The meaning of each of those expressions was deduced by careful study of the context in which each was used.)

2

Something kept scratching on the outside of the tent. I wouldn't have thought much about it if I hadn't recently seen a ridiculously melodramatic film on television in which a monster tried to get into its victim's bedroom by scratching on the door with its claw-like hands. A stupid fantasy, but it kept coming back, ruining sleep. When a cry rang out across the moor I crawled out to see what it was all about.

In a small tent this is less easy than it sounds. After extricating yourself from a cocoon-like sleeping-bag, you have to fumble with the zip-fasteners of the tent from a kneeling position.

Outside all seemed in order. The scratching noise came from clumps of spiky rushes intermittently blown by the wind against the canvas. The only explanation I have for the eerie cries is that overhead may have passed a migratory flock of stone curlews, birds which make a diabolical noise.

The moon was the colour of a corpse. Uncomforted, I crept back into the tent.

Dawn was pretty dreary, too. Flocks of drifting clouds had settled down low on the horizon, jostling each other, uneasily, like sheep undecided what to do next. Hoping fervently they would push off, I packed up and walked on, taking the left bank of the River Tavy, looking for its junction with the tributary that led to Great Kneeset. Nattor Down loomed up where it should have been, but another apparently unmapped hill popped up on the opposite side of the torrent, rather spoiling my simple conception of the landscape.

The going became difficult, for a great· deal of the stuff they call clitter, the rubble from the outcrops of granite, had fallen down into the gorge. But the compass confirmed the heading and I scrambled along as fast as I could in weather that seemed to be worsening. I decided to make for some high place where I could look around and see whether it looked safe to go on.

John Hillaby: Journey through Britain

Commentary

1 This is briskly moving narrative writing. There are descriptive, 'atmospheric' elements that are handled most effectively and unobtrusively. They help the reader to feel that he is taking part in the events, but they do not slow the pace of the narrative.

2 The use of language is well-adapted to the writer's purposes, especially the imagery and figures of speech: 'cocoon-like sleeping-bag' and 'clouds . . . like sheep . . .' are good examples.

3 The vocabulary is simple and admirably direct, always helping the reader to believe in the narrative and never getting in the way. This, the reader is made to feel, is plain, unvarnished truth. Yet there is nothing dull or predictable about the choice of words. The writer can surprise the reader with his freshness and originality: 'a hill *popped up*'; the walker is impeded by 'a great deal of *stuff* they call clitter'. *Stuff* is so surely the right word there, giving the reader the feel of the clitter *and* the walker's feelings about it; yet many writers would have been afraid to use such an 'ordinary' word. They would have struggled to find a more 'striking' word; and would not have been so effective. Those are just a few examples of Hillaby's strong writing. I'm sure you can find many more.

Typical questions and suggested answers

1 Explain why the camper could not sleep.

Answer The scratching sound on the outside of his tent reminded him of a frightening incident in a film that he had recently seen on television. (*Note on answer* It is the association of the sound with the film that keeps him awake *not* the sound itself. The correct answer takes full account of 'I wouldn't have thought much about it . . . and . . . it [the film] kept coming back, ruining sleep.' You would lose marks if you said that the scratching sound kept him awake. Nor (another trap) was it the cry that woke him. He was already awake when he heard that. It was the cry that made him decide to go outside to investigate. This particular question provides you with a good example of the precision required by comprehension questions.)

2 What was it that drove him to investigate?

Answer He left his tent when 'a cry rang out across the moor' (*Note on answer* As you have just seen in the note on Question 1 you have to keep your wits about you when answering these questions. The examiner sets them to test the accuracy of your reading. You have to get the details right. Here, a careless reader would go wrong. A careful reader sorts things out: scratching sound reminded him of film; memory of film kept him awake; cry then drove him outside to find out what was going on. Question 2 illustrates another point. It does *not* require an answer in your own words, so you are right to use the relevant quotation from the passage, since that is the quickest and most accurate way of answering. At this point revise Section 3.2 (c) and 3.3 (b)).

3 What explanations are given for the scratching sound and the cry? Answer in your own words and indicate which of the two explanations is conjectural.

Answer The writer explains the scratching sound as being caused by rushes rubbing against the tent whenever the wind blew. The cry, he says, may have been the call of stone curlews passing overhead. He is far from sure of the truth of the latter explanation. He does not put it forward as a proved fact, but offers it as a conjecture: 'The only explanation that I have . . .'; '. . . may have passed . . .'.

4 List three factors that made his journey unpleasant the next morning, supporting your answer by references to the text of the passage.

Answer These three factors made his journey unpleasant: (i) the threat of bad weather ('. . . drifting clouds had settled down low . . .'; '. . . weather that seemed to be worsening . . .'); (ii) he was not certain that he was following the right route ('. . . an apparently unmapped hill popped up . . .'); (iii) he found it hard to walk ('The going became difficult . . .').

5 State briefly what the following expressions convey to you: (i) torrent; (ii) my rather simple conception of the landscape; (iii) confirmed the heading.

Answer (i) The River Tavy, along the bank of which he was walking, is in flood. (ii) He is far from sure of his position. The sudden appearance of an unmapped hill has caused him to question the accuracy of the route that he has chosen to follow. Until the hill appeared his picture of the terrain seemed accurate. Now, it seems that he has left important features out of his picture. (*Note on that answer* You may think that it is not a brief answer, but the writer has packed a lot of meaning into 'simple conception.) (iii) He has taken a compass reading and this has assured him that he is heading in the right direction.

6 Explain in your own words the meaning of the following as used in the passage: (i) ridiculously melodramatic; (ii) stupid fantasy.

Answer Both expressions refer to the television film and both indicate that it was absurd and yet, in present circumstances, frightening. Its absurdity is conveyed by (i) 'ridiculously' and (ii) 'stupid'. Its power to frighten him is conveyed by (i) 'melodramatic' and (ii) 'fantasy'. Despite its absurdity it was preying on his fears. (*Note on answer* It was, perhaps, risky to combine the two explanations, but I hope that I made it clear to the examiner that I was taking each fully into account. I was careful to use '(i)' and '(ii)' to indicate the separate elements of my combined explanation. Each expression does, after all, refer to the same thing (the television film) and to the same qualities (its absurdity and its power to frighten). It seemed to me neat to answer as I did. You could play safer and take the two quite separately, but at the risk of some overlap and repetition in your answer. Perhaps the most useful thing about our study of this question and of ways of answering it is the demonstration of how hard one must think in order to answer comprehension questions clearly and accurately.)

7 Select three expressions that you find particularly effective in conveying an impression of the writer's fear during his uncomfortable night.

Answer   My selections are these: (i) 'claw-like hands'; (ii) 'eerie cries'; (iii) 'Uncomforted'. (*Note on answer*   Other expressions could have been chosen. Among those omitted from the suggested answer are: 'diabolical noise'; 'colour of a corpse'. The question asks for a personal choice, and one must choose. On second thoughts, I rather wish that I had chosen 'colour of a corpse'. Applied to the moon, that seems very menacing. It's as if nature itself were joining in the threat, and that is a very effective suggestion. I find the 'dead-pan' word 'Uncomforted' the most powerfully suggestive of them all. It says so much without being obviously 'vivid'. He needed comfort, for he was alone and frightened; but that one word tells the reader that he had to crawl back into his tent taking his solitude and his fear with him.

3

An hour earlier a stream of cyclists would have been turning into the main gate of Lang's. Now, at five to nine, an occasional one branched off there. The rest, a mere trickle, went on another fifty yards to the office entrance. Lawrence Spellman changed down and edged the car among them at a walking pace.

Humphrey Peart looked at the jumble of buildings and said: 'There is a certain sort of red brick that time cannot assuage. When was all this built, Lawrence?'

'Built?' said Spellman vaguely. 'It wasn't built. At least, not for us. It was just here.'

Moira Peart said: 'What's that rather intriguing bit that looks like a disused chapel?'

'A disused chapel, darling. It's still called "the chapel". We use it as a sheet metal store.'

The car nosed cautiously through the big iron gates. Lawrence said: 'This house straight ahead is where old William Lang started. It is now the offices. Then be bought a bit more and a bit more until he ended up with this bloody muddle. Those sawtooth sheds at the back are the only building on the place that was ever designed for its job. We had an American here once to see if he could help us to improve the layout. He went round the place and then came back and said:

"Gentlemen, what this place needs is a few charges of dynamite and a clean start." ' Spellman slid the car neatly into one of the white parking rectangles outside the offices. 'They say in the works that during the war Gustavus Lang used to go to chapel on Sundays and pray for the Germans to pop a bomb down on the place. Then we could have built a proper factory.' He sat for a moment looking at the irregular jumble of buildings.

Peart said with mild disbelief: 'And you come here every day?'

'That's right, Humphrey. Every day. Except Saturday, Sunday and any other day when I can find some reason not to.'

As they climbed out of the car, a shining four-and-a-half-litre Bentley drew up twenty yards away. Lawrence waved a hand vaguely towards it and the driver flapped in reply.

'Is that somebody very important?' said Peart. 'It's a very important car.'

'Jim Talbot-Rees. Sales Director. He's like that.'

Talbot-Rees had jumped out of his car and was hurrying ahead of them towards the main office door.

'Observe,' said Lawrence without malice, 'the brisk walk. The Burberry. The hat at precisely the right angle. The brief-case. It reminds you of that American advertising campaign for whisky . . . "Men of Distinction". Wouldn't you rather place an order with that, than with some scruffy little man out of a pre-war Austin Seven?'

'No,' said Peart briefly.

'Nor would I. But we're not representative.'

Nigel Balchin: *Sundry Creditors*

Commentary

1 Those are the opening paragraphs of a novel. The writer's purposes are clear: to set the scene and to introduce some of his characters. He cannot afford to waste words. He must grip his reader's attention swiftly. Novels are read for pleasure. The reader who is not interested at once is not likely to go on reading.

2 The writer's use of language is well-suited to his purposes. The sentences are short. Necessary description is quickly effected with an economical use of words. Adjectives are used sparingly. Verbs and adverbs carry the main weight of description – for example: '*edged* the car'; 'the driver *flapped* in reply'; '*slid* the car *neatly*'; 'waved a hand *vaguely*'. (We shall return to those descriptive words when discussing questions and answers on the passage. The description is not 'description for description's sake'. It is not ornament. It has work to do.) Such adjectives as are used are precise: '*sawtooth* sheds'; '*irregular* jumble of buildings'.

3 The vocabulary is simple. Only one word in the whole passage is drawn from outside the everyday range – 'assuaged' – and that plays an important part in characterising the speaker who uses it. We feel that the writer justifies its use immediately.

Typical questions and suggested answers

1 What can you deduce about Lang's from the information given in the first paragraph?

Answer Lang's is a factory. It employs quite a lot of people. It has separate entrances for its office workers and its production workers, and the office workers begin an hour later than the others. (*Note on answer* Check each item for yourself by looking for the evidence for each supplied in the first paragraph. There are other facts about Lang's elsewhere in the passage, but the question asked you to confine your answer to the first paragraph – and that is what you must do.)

2 Select two items from the passage that tell you that Lang's is badly designed for its present use.

Answer (i) Spellman describes the buildings as 'this bloody muddle'. (ii) The sheet metal is stored in a disused chapel. (*Comment on answer* There are other equally valid items that could have been used in the answer, but the question asked for two, so only two were given. For practice, select two others that tell you the same thing about Lang's.)

3 List four items about the Sales Director's appearance and behaviour to which Spellman draws attention.

Answer Spellman draws attention to (i) his 'brisk walk'; (ii) his coat ('The Burberry'); (iii) the way he wears his hat; (iv) his brief-case. (*Comment on answer* The answer illustrates the importance of doing what you are told to do. I was tempted to include the Sales Director's car in my list, for it occupies a prominent place in the description: 'a shining four-and-a-half-litre Bentley'; 'It's a very important car'. But those items are not part of Spellman's remarks and they would, therefore, be incorrect if included in this answer.)

4 How can you tell that Humphrey and Moira Peart are visitors of Lang's? Give evidence for your answer.

Answer The questions that they ask Spellman indicate that they are strangers to the place: 'When was all this built?' and 'What's that rather intriguing bit . . . ?'

5 Explain the meaning of the following as they are used in the passage: (i) assuage; (ii) sawtooth.

Answer (i) make better; make more bearable; (ii) jagged, like the teeth of a saw.

6 Describe two things that you have learnt about Spellman's character from this passage. Support your answer with brief quotations.

Answer (i) He has a dry sense of humour. His answer to Peart's question ('And you come here every day?') shows this – '. . . and any other day when I can find some reason not to'. (ii) He is a realist, trying to see things as they are. He describes Talbot-Rees objectively and 'without malice'. He recognises that the Sales Director's appearance and behaviour, though not to his liking, are an asset to Talbot-Rees in his job. ('Wouldn't you rather . . . ?' and 'Nor would I. But we're not representative.') (*Comment on answer* The passage tells us other things about Spellman's character, but I picked out the two that I found most interesting. What traits would you select as your answer to the question?)

7 Choose one example of the author's skill in using language that appeals to you and explain why you find it impressive.

Answer The author brings to life the difference in character between Lawrence Spellman and Jim Talbot-Rees. He does this swiftly and economically by his description of the contrasting manner in which each drives his car. Spellman 'edged the car among them' and 'slid the car neatly'. Talbot-Rees's car 'draws-up'. The language suggests at once that Spellman is dextrous, quietly efficient, and unostentatious, whereas Talbot-Rees is showy and self-important. (*Comment on answer* As instructed, I chose an example that I particularly liked. I could equally well have chosen the suggestive skill with which the author puts the word 'assuage' into Humphrey Peart's mouth and the way in which Peart asks Spellman a question 'with mild disbelief'. Together, those examples make an impressive demonstration of the author's skill in using language to sketch in his characters. For practice, choose and explain an example of your own.)

We move on now to full-length comprehension questions, just as you will find them in the examination paper. Work through them using the methods advised and demonstrated in the preceding sections of this chapter.

4

Read this passage carefully and then answer the questions that follow. Be sure to use your own words whenever you are instructed to do so. When you are asked to quote from the passage be careful to quote only the relevant word or words.

It may be necessary, in order that future inhabitants can enjoy clean air, that more of the cost is borne by long-term central government funds. As air pollution varies enormously from place to place and can, indeed, be very local, it may also be necessary for the central government to allocate money so that local authorities can meet special local problems. That these can be significant was shown by the report made in 1970 on behalf of the London Boroughs Association by the Greater London Council Research and Intelligence Unit. This revealed that in central London since 1958 smoke concentrations have decreased by 80 per cent, sulphur dioxide by 40 per cent, whereas sunshine has increased by 70 per cent and winter visibility has improved threefold. There have been reductions in mortality and hospital admissions associated with air pollution and in the response to it of bronchitis, as well as clear if less documented increases in plant types and bird species in the cities. The cost of all this has been roughtly 30p per head per annum. Truly this is a great social benefit in return for very little cost.

It is essential that local government authorities regard the quality of the air as one of their major responsibilities. Such authorities can usually contribute a great deal through their various committees for public health, housing and town and country planning. They can obviously plan zones for industries by relating them to climatic and other geographic factors. They can develop district heating schemes and low-density housing or high-density flats. In particular, they can plan their towns in relation to the traffic they must withstand. Air must be 'planned' if its quality is to be ensured.

This leads on to the main goal, which is to reduce substantially and in time cut out air pollution at source. Future generations will recognise this - as with most pollution - as waste of recyclable resources. And with proper planning, particularly of energy, it should be unnecessary. The atmosphere - as with the rest of nature - is a dynamic system. It has dealt with much natural pollution - volcanoes, earthquakes, etc - in excess of man's efforts to date by a process of continuous recycling. But this capacity to cleanse itself could be impaired, as has happened with some rivers and lakes, and this must be prevented. Hence the need to know of any substantial or potentially harmful emissions. This is possible. Industrialists, for example, could be required to report all discharges into the atmosphere as they do with those into water or dumping on land. Increasingly, our wastes are incinerated and blown into the atmosphere; more and more we use dangerous substances with a long active life, some of which can have harmful interactions or become concentrated for too long in one place.

Man is always interfering with nature, sometimes intentionally, sometimes accidentally or unconsciously. Air pollution is obviously not intended, but that does not make its effects any less serious and man should act consciously to control it. Air pollution may, in the long term, cause an imbalance in the environment which exceeds the interferences or controls deliberately imposed by man.

Robert Arvill: *Man and Environment*

1 Quote from paragraph 1 the words that give the author's reasons for his belief that central government may have to provide money to enable local authorities to meet their special problems.

2 Explain in your own words the meaning of each of the following expressions as used in the passage: (i) documented; (ii) zones; (iii) district heating schemes; (iv) high-density; (v) recyclable; (vi) dynamic; (vii) impaired; (viii) emissions; (ix) incinerated; (x) interactions.

3 What evidence does the writer give to support his claim that a great social benefit has been achieved in return for very little cost (see paragraph 1)?

4 At the beginning of paragraph 3 the author describes 'the main goal'. State in your own words what he means by that.

5 What two examples of 'natural pollution' does the writer name in paragraph 3?

6 What two sources of pollution are industrialists already required to report?

7 Explain in you own words the long-term danger that is described in the last paragraph.

5

Read this passage carefully and then answer the questions, taking care to follow exactly the instructions accompanying each.

When I went round in the morning to visit her, I found myself met by a certain unhelpful stalling. The lady in charge, a lady in white whose title was not clear to me, assured me that all was well, that all was progressing most satisfactorily, that the child was as comfortable as could be expected. 'I'd like to go and see her,' I said then, summoning up a little courage.

'I'm afraid that won't be possible,' said the lady in white with calm certainty, looking down at her file of notes.

'Why not? I said. 'I would like to see her, I know she'd like to see me.'

The lady in white embarked upon a long explanation about upsetting children, upsetting mothers, upsetting other children, upsetting other mothers, justice to all, disturbing the nurses' routine, and such topics. As she talked, in her smooth even tones, all kinds of memories filtered back into my mind, memories of correspondences in *The Times* and *The Guardian* upon this very subject, composed of letters from mothers like myself who had not been allowed in. 'What about visiting hours?' I said, and back came the civil, predictable answer,

'I'm afraid that for such small infants we don't allow any visiting time at all. We really do find that it causes more inconvenience to staff and patients than we can possibly cope with. Really, Mrs Stacey, you must understand that it is no practical use to visit such a young child, she will settle much more happily if she doesn't see you. You'd be amazed to see how soon they settle down. Mothers never believe us, but we know from experience how right we are to make this regulation.'

I didn't like the sound of that word 'settle': it suggested a settling into lethargy and torpor, such as I remembered to have read of in *The Times*. Octavia had never been settled in her short life, and I did not want her to begin now. Already, in twenty-four hours, we had endured the longest separation of our lives, and I began to see it stretching away, indefinitely prolonged. Also, because they would not let me see the child, I suspected that they had not told me the whole truth about her recovery; was there now in her small countenance something too dreadful for me to behold? I voiced this fear, feeling that it would have some effect, and be at least appreciated.

'I can't believe until I see her', I said, 'that everything really is all right. I just can't believe it.

She took my point. 'Mrs Stacey,' she said, looking up and meeting with straight, woman-to-woman frankness my anxious gaze, 'you must believe me when I say that I have given you all the information there is about your daughter. We are making no attempt to conceal anything from you because there is nothing to conceal. Mr Protheroe expressed personal satisfaction at the progress of the operation and is calling in this morning to check on progress. If you would like to see his report, here it is.'

And she detached a piece of paper from the file marked Not to Be Seen By Patient and pushed it over to me. I glanced at it, but could see it was nothing but a mass of technicalities, so I did not try to read it. I felt better, though, by virture of the fact that she had let me look, for she could not reasonably have relied upon the exact extent of my ignorance. By this time it was quite easy to tell from her expression that she considered I was nothing but an ordinary and tedious time-waster, and as I dislike being any such thing, and as I could see that I was making no progress, I decided that I had no choice but to leave gracefully, so I did.

Margaret Drabble: *The Millstone*

1   What is the name of the person who tells the story? How do you know?
2   Two other people are named in the passage. Give their names and explain briefly who you think each is.

3 The fourth character is not named. Quote from the passage one description of that character as given by the narrator.

4 Can you think of a reason why the author does not name that character? Does the fact that the character is left anonymous add anything to the characterisation and atmosphere of the story?

5 What is the job of the unnamed character? Quote briefly from the passage in support of your answer.

6 Give a word or phrase similar in meaning to each of the following as used in the passage: (i) 'stalling' (paragraph 1); (ii) 'embarked upon' (paragraph 4); (iii) 'a mass of technicalities' (paragraph 9); (iv) 'tedious' (paragraph 9); (v) 'gracefully' (paragraph 9).

7 Contrast the different attitudes of the two main characters as revealed in (i) 'summoning up a little courage' and (ii) 'with calm certainty' (paragraphs 1 and 2).

8 What does the expression 'embarked upon a long explanation' paragraph 4) tell you about the narrator's thoughts and feelings at that moment?

9 What is it possible to deduce about the narrator's educational background? Refer to the words in the passage that support your answer.

10 Explain what the narrator means by 'the exact extent of my ignorance' (paragraph 9).

11 Describe in your own words two features of the narrator's character that are revealed in the passage. Refer briefly to the evidence on which you base your answer.

3.5 MULTIPLE-CHOICE QUESTIONS

Some examining boards test comprehension by setting objective or multiple-choice tests. The tests are called 'objective' because they are designed to eliminate the marker's personal ('subjective') judgement of the merit of the candidate's answer. This, in theory at least, provides an entirely fair and accurate way of measuring the candidate's ability to comprehend.

The passage set for study is followed by a number of questions to each of which four or five answers are provided, only *one* of which is correct. The candidate has to select the correct answer and indicate his choice by writing its identification in the space provided on the answer sheet. Beyond that, he is not called upon to do any writing.

A multiple-choice comprehension test is set out like this:

Read the following passage carefully, then read the instructions printed after it.
[Passage follows here]

Read the passage again. Then answer the questions. Each question has been given four suggested answers. Select in each case the answer that you think is best and mark the answer sheet with your choice.

1 The expression 'the derisory total of less than 10,000 houses' (ll. – to –) refers to

A the houses demolished by the development scheme
B the poor building standards on the new estate
C the results of the ill-considered Housing Act described in paragraph 1
D the shortage of skilled workers in the construction industry

It is not possible, of course, to decide on the best answer in the sample choices given above. Without the passage to study nobody can choose sensibly from those alternative answers.

That sample layout of an objective or multiple-choice test was provided to familiarise you with the method used and to emphasise the fact that you do not have to write out your answers. You simply mark the answer sheet 1 '*A*' or 1 '*B*', or whatever is appropriate to the choice that you have made. Because no writing is demanded, more questions (20 or so) are usually set in multiple-choice questions than in the other kind.

It must be remembered, however, that multiple-choice tests demand from the candidate the same concentrated, imaginative reading of the set passage on which they are based as do the more orthodox types of comprehension tests that we have been studying and practising earlier in this chapter.

CHAPTER 4

SUMMARY

4.1 THE IMPORTANCE OF SUMMARY

Summary of one kind or another is required by all the examining boards and, whether it is based on the comprehension passage or on a separate passage, the summary exercise carries a high proportion of the total marks. A good performance in this branch of English language work is crucial to success in the examination as a whole.

The importance that the examiners attach to summary reflects its importance in everyday life. It is one of the mental activities in which we are all frequently involved, whether we realise it or not.

A few examples will readily illustrate how often the need to summarise occurs. A letter arrives for you from a firm to which you have applied for a job. As you are reading it, your mother asks, 'What do they say?' She is asking for a summary. So is somebody who comes into the room half-way through a news item on television and says, 'What's that all about?'

More obviously, a summary is required when, at work, your boss pushes a newspaper across to you and says, 'There's a report on page four of objections to the council's outline development plan. Let me have the gist of it by lunchtime. I'm meeting the borough surveyor at 2.30, and those arguments may bear on our proposed extension to the paint shop.'

Thus, the summaries required in the examination are a way of testing skills that you need in daily life.

4.2 THE SKILLS INVOLVED

Summary involves all the skills required for general competence in the use of language. Far from being an artificial exercise designed by examiners as a test for candidates, it is an accurate measure of your *ability to communicate*. It tests you in comprehension and in composition, demanding:

- first – that you can understand what you read;
- second – that you can express that understanding.

Comprehension and the best method of setting about it were discussed and practised in Chapter 3. As was pointed out there, the initial stages of grasping the meaning of a set passage are also the initial stages of preparing to summarise that passage. You will need, therefore, to refer to Sections 3.1 and 3.2 as you work through this chapter.

For the moment, we will assume that you have completed the comprehension of the passage that you are about to summarise. Here is a breakdown of the skills that are needed, whether you are required to make a summary of the whole passage or of selected parts:

- the ability to *organise* your answer in a *coherent* and *logical* manner;
- that, in turn, requires competence in *sentence* and *paragraph* construction and a thorough knowledge of punctuation;
- the possession of, and the judgement to make use of, a large *vocabulary*, so that you can *condense* the passage that you are summarising and choose *appropriate* words to reflect its spirit and its writer's intentions.

Each of those requirements is discussed later in this chapter.

4.3 DIFFERENT KINDS OF SUMMARY

(a) Précis or full-length summary

Précis is a synonym for 'summary'. The word 'précis' came into the English language from French. It is useful to bear in mind that, in French, when *précis* is used as a noun it means 'summary', and when it is used as an adjective it means 'precise, accurate, definite'.

For that is what a précis is: a precise, accurate summary – and it is 'definite' in the sense that it *must* be written to the *exact* word length stipulated in the examiner's instructions.

When précis is required in the examination the instructions generally follow a well-established pattern. A separate passage is usually set and the candidate is instructed to reduce that passage to a third of its length (in the case of longer passages) or to a quarter of its length (in the case of shorter passages). Usually, the permitted number of words is stated: 'not more than 300 of your own words'; 'in about 200 of your own words'. When an approximate word length is given you should aim at being not more than five words above or below the stated figure.

Nowadays, we tend to use 'précis' to describe the summary of a whole passage, and to use the word 'summary' for the kind of selective summary and the short summary questions that most examining boards now set.

Typical précis instructions
Make a précis (summary) of the following passage in not more than 150 words. You may have to retain some words or brief expressions from the original passage but, as far as possible, *use your own words*. State at the end of your précis the exact number of words that you have used. There are 455 words in the original passage.

(b) Selective summary
Instead of being asked to summarise a whole passage the candidate is instructed to select from its contents the items that bear upon a specified subject and to summarise those.

The set passage may deal with two main themes, and the instructions may require a summary of one of the two. For example, in a passage describing the progress of an invention from the laboratory to commercial use the subject-matter may divide into an account of the early experiments and the development of those to the production stage, followed by an account of the way in which, and with what success, the product was marketed. The candidate may be asked to summarise one or the other.

A less straightforward exercise will involve the selection and summarising of material that is found here and there throughout the set passage. For example, an account of a politician's life may include references to various periods of his career during which his particular qualities of character and temperament were exercised in different ways and with varying degrees of success. The candidate may be asked to select and summarise those qualities that were either of enduring advantage or of sporadic disadvantage to him.

As those illustrations show, the examiner is testing the candidate's ability to 'see through' the material and to reach the heart of the matter *as specified in his instructions*. Much that is important in the original has to be disregarded in the summary because it is *irrelevant* to the job that the candidate has been told to do.

Again, the material for selective summarising may not be a single passage of continuous prose. It may take the form of a conversation, or of a series of letters, or of notes or memoranda.

But, whatever the form, the candidate will be clearly instructed what aspect of the subject-matter to select and how many words to use.

Typical instructions for selective summary
1 Study this discussion. Then, in one paragraph of not more than 80 of your own words, summarise the speakers' views on corporal punishment

in schools. (N.B. The speakers may discuss other subjects, too - school uniform, compulsory games, the school curriculum, etc. - and they may have interesting and important things to say about them all. Those other subjects have no place in your summary, which must be concerned *only* with the subject specified in the instructions.)

2 Study this correspondence between Mr Brown and the Westshire County Planning Officer. Then, in one paragraph of about 100 words, summarise the points at issue over access to the garage, for the building of which Mr Brown is seeking planning permission. Use your own words as far as possible, though it may be necessary to employ some of the technical terms used in the letters. (N.B. Other subjects may well be discussed - colours, kinds of doors, building materials, etc. - but they are not relevant to the summary that has been specified.)

(c) Short summary questions

These are a particular kind of selective summary. They occur among - and as part of - the comprehension questions set on the given passage. They do not differ *in kind* from any other exercises in summary, for they involve the same kind of mental processes and the application of the same skills. But they do not always contain the instruction 'summarise', and this can confuse an ill-prepared candidate.

You can recognise that they *are* exercises in summary by the number of words permitted in the answer. Whereas a comprehension question can be answered briefly, the answer to a summary question is allowed (and expected) to contain more words. Also, of course, more marks are given for a summary question than for a single comprehension question. Some examining boards indicate on the examination paper the marks given for each question. Whether your board follows that practice or nor, you may be sure that examiners will allot more marks to a question requiring, say, a 60- or 70-word answer than to one that can be answered in one word, or one phrase, or one short sentence.

Typical short summary question

Note This example is presented in the kind of context in which it would be found in an examination paper. It is accompanied by 'straight' comprehension questions. Read the passage carefully and then answer the questions. Be sure to use your own words wherever you are instructed to do so. When you are asked to quote from the passage be careful to quote only the relevant word or words.

[Passage follows here.]

1 Quote from the first paragraph the two words that indicate that the narrator was nervous. (4 marks)

2 Give one word meaning the same or nearly the same as the following as used in the passage: (i) devious (l. -); (ii) premature (l. -). (2 marks)

3 Set out clearly, and in not more than 60 *of your own words*, the reasons that Jan gives for being suspicious of Blenkinson. (10 marks)

4 Write down two of the things that you learn about Henry Jones's previous career. Indicate briefly the evidence on which your answer is based. (4 marks)

[Question 3, above, is a short summary question.]

4.4 PRACTICE IN PRÉCIS

Although only a minority of the examining boards test candidates in summary by setting full-length summary of a whole passage, a study of précis is the best way to learn how to summarise. All the skills demanded by every kind of summary are involved in the making of a précis.

(a) Getting the gist of it

When (in Section 3.2) you were studying comprehension a method of reading was advised. Exactly the same approach is required when you are setting about the making of a précis, since comprehension is an essential preliminary to summarising.

Revise Section 3.2 now, paying close attention to the reading method described there. Note especially the importance of writing out a brief statement of the gist of the passage. Study again the examples of 'encapsulating' statements, noting how each goes to the heart of the matter, *condensing* into a very few words what the passage is chiefly about.

Making a clear, brief statement *in your own words* of the gist of the passage is the first stage.

(b) The spirit of the passage and the writer's intentions

With your statement of its chief theme in mind you now work through the passage, attempting to deepen your understanding of it.

As you read, you note key words, phrases, and sentences that indicate the spirit in which the passage was written and the author's intentions when writing it.

You can note these key expressions either by underlining them in the passage or by jotting them down on your rough paper.

If, as you read, you ask yourself these two questions you will pick out the key points:

- *What* is the writer trying to do?
- *How* is he using language to achieve his aims?

Reading like that is 'reading between the lines' (3.2). The reader is entering into the writer's mind and perceiving his intentions.

This is the second stage of précis. Let us see how it works. Suppose that the passage you are preparing to précis is an account of the invention of gunpowder. You have completed the second stage of your work when you have answers to these questions:

- Is this a 'scientific' account of the invention, employing technical terms and written for a special readership?

or

- Is this a 'popular' account of the invention, written in language that anybody can understand?
- Does the writer simply give an account of the invention?

or

- Does he introduce other topics?
- Does he write about the effects of the invention?
- Does he say whether he thinks that it was a beneficial or a harmful invention?
- Does he give reasons for his opinions and, if so, what are they?

Asking (and answering) such questions provides you with a full understanding of what the writer was doing. Once you have that deep understanding you know what ground your précis must cover.

(c) The structure of the passage

Stage three of your work is an analysis of the structure of the passage. In stages one and two you discovered what the passage is about and what the writer was trying to do. Now, in stage three, you take the passage to pieces, noting the steps by which it passes *from* its beginning *through* its middle *to* its end.

Of course, you will not include in your précis everything that the passage contains, nor will you necessarily present the items in your précis in the same order as that in which they occur in the original.

You have to *condense* to write a précis. To condense, you have to:

- omit any material that is not essential to the main theme;

and

- save words, by reducing longer expressions to shorter ones with equivalent meanings (a point developed later in this chapter).

Your précis must also present its summary of the main theme of the original in a *coherent* and *logical* way. When you are shortening the subject you may find that you need to rearrange the order in which the items occur in the original. An order that is satisfactory in the longer original *may* be unsuitable for your shortened version.

But, until you have noted all the items included in the original and the order in which those items are presented, you cannot decide what to include in your précis or in what order to present the items that you have selected.

(d) Stages 1–3 in action

The passage chosen for this demonstration is short, because I want to make the method as clear as possible; but, as we shall see later, it works just as well with longer passages.

> Henry Ford did more than any other man to make the motor car a popular and readily available means of transport. He was not an inventor, and he contributed nothing to the scientific evolution of the car; but he was a genius who applied the principles of mass-production to the making of cars, and so transformed what had been the sport and pleasure of the few into a useful vehicle for the many. Ford decided that cars must be tough enough to stand up to daily wear and tear on ordinary roads; that they must become cheap enough to be within the reach of ordinary people; that their construction must be simplified so that spare parts could be widely available and easily fitted. These aims were realised in his huge factories, where mechanised and highly organised car production was first undertaken.

Stage 1   Statement of gist of passage
Henry Ford's unique contribution to the development of the motor car.

Stage 2   Spirit of passage and writer's intentions
Writer gives a straightforward account of Ford's historical importance in development of car, and of methods he used to make the changes he brought about. No value judgements made by writer – concerned only with facts.

Stage 3   Analysis of structure of passage
One paragraph, the structure of which is:

Main point 1   Henry Ford . . . means of transport.
　　　　　　　　1(a) . . . not an inventor
　　　　　　　　1(b) . . . contributed nothing to scientific evolution . . .
Main point 2   . . . genius . . . principles of mass production . . . cars.
　　　　　　　　2(a) . . . transformed . . . sport and pleasure of the few . . .
　　　　　　　　　　　useful vehicle for the many.
Main point 3   Ford decided that cars must be
　　　　　　　　3(a) . . . tough enough . . .

3(b) ... cheap enough ...

3(c) ... spare parts ... widely available ... easily fitted.

Main point 4 These aims were realised ... first undertaken.

As you see Stage 3 produces a 'skeleton' of the original passage. You dissect the passage and lay bare the bones of its structure.

(e) Selecting the key points

This is Stage 4. With the skeleton in front of you, you can decide what items to include in your précis and the order in which you will present those items.

To guide your selection refer to your brief statement of the gist of the passage (Stage 1). Items that are directly relevant to that statement *may* be included in your précis: any that are not *must* be excluded.

When, as often happens, an item has relevance to the main theme of the passage but seems of minor importance, you can usually decide whether to include it or not by referring to the writer's purposes, as discovered in Stage 2. An item may bear on the main theme but be of comparatively small importance to the writer's chief intentions in writing the passage. It has a part to play in the original, where the writer was free from the pressure on space that you have to contend with. You are looking to save words, so a doubtful item that does not seem to be essential to the writer's purposes must be excluded.

Applying those considerations to the passage 'skeletonised' in 4.4(d) we find that the key points are: 1-2-3-3(a)-3(b)-3(c).

Those key items – and only those – will be included in the précis.

It is instructive to study the omitted items and the reasons for their exclusion.

Points 1(a) and 1(b) are excluded. The writer's chief intention in the passage is to describe what Henry Ford did – to emphasise his positive achievement, *not* to dwell on the qualities that he did not possess.

Point 2(a) is excluded. Its substance is adequately represented (for the précis-writer's purposes) in 1.

Point 4 is excluded. It is an expansion of 2. It makes a useful 'rounding off' for the original passage, but it is not a sufficiently separate and distinctive item to merit inclusion in the précis.

(f) Making a plan for the précis

When you have decided on the key points you are ready to write out a plan in note form from which you can write your précis. This is Stage 5.

Bear the following advice in mind as you make your notes:

- use *your own words* as far as possible;

- include sufficient detail to enable you to write the *first draft* of the précis *from your notes* and without referring to the original passage.

There are two good reasons behind that advice. First, if you use the writer's words (instead of your own) in your notes you will be in danger of incorporating them in your précis. Second, if your notes are too thin and you have to keep referring to the original as you write your first draft, you will be in danger of departing from the scheme of key points worked out in stage four. You will then lose sight of the priorities and scale of relevance that govern the inclusion or exclusion of items. The resulting muddle will ruin your précis.

(g) Recap – the first five stages in précis-writing

Stage 1 Study the subject matter of the original passage. Discover its gist. State its gist in your own words.

Stage 2 Discover the writer's purposes. Get clear in your own mind what he was intending to do.

Stage 3 Analyse the structure of the passage, noting the separate items and the order in which they are presented. Make a skeleton of the passage.

Stage 4 Decide which items are fundamental to the writer's theme and purpose. List those key points.

Stage 5 Use your list of key points as the framework for a *detailed* plan on which to write the first draft of your précis. Check each item in your plan to make sure that it is an accurate representation of the item in the original to which it corresponds. Use your own words wherever possible throughout your plan.

(h) Pruning and polishing the first draft

Having written your first draft from your précis plan you have still got a lot of work to do before you can write out on your answer sheet a fair copy of your final version. This is what must be done when first draft is complete.

(i) Count the number of words in your first draft. You will almost always find that you have exceeded the permitted word limit. So, usually, the first thing to do is *prune*. (N.B. If you find that your first draft is comfortably under the permitted length, do not be comforted! That is a danger signal. You have almost certainly omitted essential points from the original passage.)

(ii) Check that your draft is a *connected and readable composition*. A précis is a shortened version of the original, but it is not to be written in note form or in a series of jerky sentences. Nor should its style be informal. Avoid all colloquialisms and slang.

(iii) Check for errors in punctuation, spelling and grammar.

(iv) Check that you have provided a suitable title.

(v) Check that you have stated *accurately* the number of words used in your précis. The examiner has a pretty good idea of how many words occupy how may lines of the answer sheet. If the number you state at the end makes him suspicious, he will count every word in your précis, and he will not be pleased at being put to the trouble.

When all that pruning and polishing has been completed you are ready to write the final version on the answer sheet.

Set out in its successive stages and discussed in detail, the writing of a précis seems a time-consuming and daunting task. 'How can I possibly get through all that in the exam?' you may be saying. Well, you must - and you *can*.

Remember that method is essential - and the method that has been set out here is a well-tried and successful one. To attempt to write a précis (or any other kind of summary) 'off the cuff' is to court disaster.

Remember, too, that describing the successive steps and illustrating how they work takes longer than actually carrying them out.

Above all, remember that regular practice in preparation for the examination will speed you up. You should practise précis-writing, using the method set out here, once a week during your examination preparation. Then you will answer your summary question with confidence and efficiency. You will also find that this regular summary practice brings about an improved performance in every other branch of your English Language work. (And that, of course, means that your work in all subjects will improve.)

I shall now work through a complete précis to show you how to apply the method advocated in this book. Pay close attention to the comments on the various stages. They are meant to take you right into the workshop.

(i) Worked example of précis, with a commentary

Note A short passage has been chosen so that each stage can be fully discussed and illustrated within the space available in this chapter. Short though the passage is, the exercise is an example of full-length summary (or précis), since the summariser (the précis-writer) is instructed to deal with the contents of the whole passage.

Summarise the following passage in not more than 65 words. You may have to employ some words or brief expressions from the original passage but, as far as possible, *use your own words*. State at the end of your précis the exact number of words that it contains. There are 250 words in the original passage. Provide your précis with a suitable title. The words of the title do *not* count towards the word total permitted.

Stanley Spencer never looked on his writing as something private; he intended to publish what he wrote. His autobiography was to be a fulfilment and rounding-off of his painting. But as a writer he lacked the discipline which made composition the outstanding feature of his painting. He wrote with wonderful freshness, but could not cut or select or prune; everything was of equal importance. When Maurice Collis received the two trunks and the large wooden box on castors containing these papers he was appalled. To read every word, let alone sort, select and arrange in chronological order this mountain of papers which, taken out of their trunks, filled an entire room, seemed at first an impossible task.

With the help of his daughter, a writer herself and used to research, he set to work. Often he worked seven days a week and sometimes late at night, not because he was being pressed by his publishers, but because he found the material engrossing. The occasional reports he sent at this time were all the more interesting because we knew that he was not a man of gushing or even ready enthusiasm. A selection of these bulletins reads:

'Stanley Spencer is a wonderful original, a far more remarkable man than I supposed before I read the papers.'

'The drama increases the more one reads.'

'New and extraordinary material goes on appearing.'

'The whole of Stanley Spencer's life is revealed in his pictures if one has the key.'

Irene Stirling: 'The Spencer Papers' (from *The Bookseller*)

Stage 1   statement of main theme (gist) of passage
The enormous quantity of Stanley Spencer's writing gave Maurice Collis (his biographer) a difficult and laborious task, which he tackled with enthusiasm because the material fascinated him.

Comments
1 I had to decide whether the subject matter of the first four sentences of the original made a major contribution to the theme. In the end I decided that their contents were *introductory* to the main theme. It was *because* of Spencer's qualities as a writer, as set out in the first four sentences, that he produced such an enormous quantity of papers. The fact that matters (to the précis writer working on this passage) is that he *did* produce so much (not *why* he produced so much) and that, in consequence, Maurice Collis was faced with a huge task.

2 I had to decide what Maurice Collis's role was, since that is not directly stated in the original. Careful 'reading between the lines' revealed that he was writing a life of Spencer. Evidence: (i) Spencer 'intended to

publish what he wrote'. Something – presumably death – has prevented him from doing so. Consequently, his *autobiography* will not be written, but a *biography* is being prepared. (ii) Maurice Collis received all the Spencer papers, which he had to 'read . . . sort, select and arrange in chronological order'. That is a description of the task of a biographer. (iii) Collis is working for publishers (see second paragraph of passage). (iv) All of Collis's 'bulletins' (quoted at the end) refer to aspects of Spencer's life, work, and personality, so he is obviously discovering all that he possibly can about the man.

Stage 2   the writer's purpose
To communicate two things to the reader as vividly as possible: (i) the enormous labour that faced Collis; (ii) the enthusiasm with which he undertook that labour, fired by the fascination of the material.

Stage 3   skeleton outline of contents of original
    1 Spencer's qualities as a writer
    1(a) did not see his writing as private – intended to publish
    1(b) importance he attached to his proposed autobiography – fulfilment of his painting
    1(c) an undisciplined writer
    1(d) a fresh and lively writer, incapable of selecting and pruning
    2 Enormous quantity of papers received by Collis
    2(a) Collis's initial reaction – 'he was appalled'
    2(b) task of reading and sorting papers seemed impossible
    3 His daughter, experienced writer and researcher, helped him – he got down to it
    3(a) Ceaseless labour – '. . . seven days a week and sometimes late at night . . .'
    3(b) Labour sustained because material was engrossing
    4 His 'bulletins' to his publishers quoted to illustrate his enthusiasm for work

Stage 4   key points selected from skeleton
Before selecting key points I referred to my statement of the main theme and my description of the writer's intentions. Guided by those I decided that the following were the key points: 2–2(a)–2(b)–3–3(a)–3(b)

Stage 5   a detailed plan for the précis
    1 Spencer's papers filled two trunks and a large wooden box on castors when they reached Maurice Collis, his biographer.
    1(a) Collis horrified at first by sheer bulk of material.

1(b) Task of reading, sorting, selecting, and arranging in chronological order all those papers seemed impossible.

2 Aided by his daughter, an experience writer and researcher, he got down to work.

2(a) He had to work extremely hard - every day and late at night.

2(b) He was sustained in his labours because - as his reports to his publishers showed - he found the Spencer material engrossing.

Comments

1 I was not entirely happy with that plan when I had finished it. I felt that I had got the order of the précis right, but I was not too sure that the balance of the contents was an accurate reflection of the key points that I had selected. I knew, too, that - here and there - I had copied words from the original. Consequently, I was uncomfortable about one or two of the expressions in the plan and knew that I ought to find substitutes for them.

2 However, since I was aware of the weaknesses in the plan, I decided to go ahead with my first draft, working entirely from my notes. Then, when I knew what pruning had to be done, I could pay special attention to balance and vocabulary, checking back with the original passage.

Stage 6 first draft of précis

Spencer's writing was not very disciplined, and his papers filled two trunks and a large wooden box on castors when they reached his biographer, Maurice Collis. They filled a whole room when they were unpacked.

At first, Collis was horrified by the sheer bulk of the material. The task of reading, sorting, selecting, and arranging in chronological order all those papers seemed impossible. With the help of his daughter, an experienced writer and researcher, he got down to work. He had to work extremely hard every day and late into the night. He was sustained in his immense labours because - as his reports to his publishers showed - he found the Spencer material engrossing.

Stage 7 pruning and polishing the first draft

1 *The word count* showed that I had used nearly double the number of words allowed! There were 113 words in my first draft, and the instructions stipulated not more than 65. A most thorough revision was clearly essential.

2 *Pruning* involves two operations: (i) Strike out material that is irrelevant to the main theme; strike out material that plays no major part in achieving the writer's purposes. (ii) Substitute brief expressions where longer ones have been used. Try especially to find single compendious words to take the place of phrases (*compendious* means 'containing the

substance within small compass'). The précis writer needs a large vocabulary, with the aid of which he can make one word in his précis do the work of several words in the original.

3 *Pruning the contents of the first draft.* I looked at the first paragraph of my draft, then compared it with my précis plan and with the original. I'd slipped up there. The point about Spencer's writing was *not* included in my plan. Obviously, I had allowed a memory of the original passage to upset the balance of my key point selection as I wrote the first draft.

Again, why include those details about the trunks and the wooden box on castors? They appeared in my plan. This was one of its faults, for I certainly had not the space to include details in the précis. In the original, those details provide a vivid illustration of the massive quantity of the Spencer papers, but the précis-writer cannot afford to include illustrative details. He has to concentrate on the bare essentials. In any case, I had made the necessary point by using the words 'sheer bulk' in the second paragraph of my draft.

Another reference to my key points showed that, in the draft, I had spent far too long in getting to the first main point. It was apparent to me now that I must cut right through the first paragraph of the draft – probably discard it – and get at 'the meat' of the précis straight away.

I then revised the opening to read:

> Maurice Collis, the biographer of Stanley Spencer, was horrified by the sheer bulk of the material when the huge collection of Spencer's papers reached him.

What other material could be struck out? I had achieved a much crisper and better balanced opening for my précis, but I saved only 22 words. Where else had I used unnecessary details?

An obvious example occurs in paragraph two of my draft, where the statement 'He had to work extremely hard every day and late into the night' says far more than is needed. The point to be made is that the biographer had to work extremely hard. The précis-writer does not have to *prove* the point by using details.

On checking with the original, I found that I had not been accurate in my use of those space-wasting words. The original does *not* say that he worked every day and late into the night. It says that he *often* worked seven days a week and *sometimes* late at night. So, I had used unnecessary details, consumed precious words, *and* I had committed the worst fault that a précis-writer can commit – I had distorted the meaning of the original passage.

Next, I realised that the material in parentheses in the last sentence of my draft was unnecessary. Again, I was using details to illustrate or prove facts that, as a précis-writer, I needed only to state. The point that the précis must make is that Collis's enthusiasm saw him through the heavy task. There is no need to waste words in explaining how that enthusiasm was made plain to the publishers.

Finally, I considered whether the material about the biographer's daughter was necessary ('. . . herself an experienced writer and researcher . . .'). I decided that it served a useful purpose in the précis, for the fact that he had to have help emphasises the laborious nature of his task, and the fact that he needed skilled help backs up the statement that it was a difficult task. Also, I had reworded the original, turning 'a writer herself and used to research' into an equivalent expression in my own words.

4 *Word-pruning and substitution in the first draft.* I saw that I had used words wastefully in my first draft. In the second paragraph 'The task of reading, sorting, selecting, and arranging in chronological order' is almost a transposition from the original and it is very word-consuming. Surely I could think of a compendious word to do the work that those words do? What does the expression 'sorting, selecting, and arranging in chronological order' mean in this context? It means *editing*. So, one word does the work of seven. *And* I was now using my own language instead of words copied for the original.

Again, I noticed that I had lifted the word 'engrossing' straight out of the original passage. It is a key word, so I had to find a word of my own that meant the same - or nearly the same - and the use of which would show my reader that I had understood one of the main points made by the original. I thought of 'fascinating' (which I had already used in Stage 1) but it did not seem quite right. It gave a sense of the attraction that the material had for the biographer, but it did not convey the sense of being totally immersed in the task - of being willingly 'up to the neck in it'. It is important that the précis should reflect the spirit of the orignal, so I wanted to do better than 'fascinating'. In the end, I decided that 'absorb' and 'engross' were truly equivalent in this context.

State 8   writing the final version

By now, I felt that I had been as critical of my own first draft as the examiner would have been had he seen it. I hoped that I had identified its chief faults. I had used my knowledge of précis-writing technique in my attempt to improve the draft. I could move on to my final version.

> Maurice Collis, the biographer of Stanley Spencer, was horrified by the sheer bulk of the material when the huge collection of Spencer's papers reached him. Even just to read them all, let alone edit them, seemed impossible. With the help of his daughter, herself an experienced writer and researcher, he worked hard and

long, sustained in his immense labours by his absorption in his subject.

(65 words)

There are, as you see, exactly 65 words in the final version, so the examiner's word limit has been complied with.

The précis seems to me to be accurate, to cover the main points made in the original passage, and to accord with the purposes that the writer had in mind.

It is, I think, a clear and connected piece of writing, and its style is appropriate.

All in all, it is now as good as I can make it in the time available.

Stage 9   fair copy and title for précis
All that remains to be done is to write out a fair copy on the answer sheet, *remembering to provide a suitable title for the précis*.

The test for a good précis is this:

● Would a reader of this précis *who had not seen the original passage* learn from the précis all the *essential* material contained in the original?

That test indicates what kind of a title you must provide for a précis.

The précis title must give the *source* of the material that has been summarised. If the précis title does not provide the source of the original material then essential information is withheld from the reader of the précis.

So, in the case of the précis just completed, the title is:

Précis of an extract from 'The Spencer Papers' by Irene Stirling (from *The Bookseller*).

Notes on précis titles
1 The précis title should contain *full* details of the source, as provided by the original material. Typical examples of précis titles are:

Précis of Chapter 2, *The Economics of the Village*, by R. K. Penny: The Mint Press, 1980.
Précis of an extract from Chapter 6, *By Land, Sea and Air*, by J. Wheelwright: Smith, Brown & Co., 1973: from 'Transport breakdowns persist . . .' (p. 198) to '. . . a feature of the diesel engine.' (p. 200).
Précis of correspondence between Mr L. T. Jones, Managing Director, Agricrops Ltd, and Principal Secretary, Trading Division, Ministry of Agriculture: 3 February 1969–10 November 1979.

2 See Chapter 7 for a discussion of the punctuation used in those examples.

4.5 SELECTIVE SUMMARY

Practice in making full-length summaries, using the techniques described and illustrated in this chapter, will give you the confidence and experience that you need to answer selective summary questions. The same principles apply to both: only the scale of the operation is different.

The instructions for selective summaries direct your attention to a part (or parts) of the subject-matter, whereas in making a précis you take the whole of the subject-matter as your field of operations.

Of course, you cannot make a successful selective summary until you have studied the *whole* passage carefully, because you need to identify the selected area, picking out what concerns you and excluding what does not.

You also need to have a good understanding of the whole passage in order to understand fully each part of it. Words, sentences, and paragraphs take a large part of their meaning from the whole of their context, not just from their immediate surroundings. (See Chapters 5 and 6.)

Nevertheless, it is important to be clear that you are instructed to operate on different areas of the original passage when selective summary is called for.

- When making a précis you identify and then present in your own words and in shortened form *the major points of the main theme* in the passage *as a whole*.
- When making a selective summary you identify and then present in your own words and in shortened form *the major points* made in *a specified part* of the passage. *Or* you may be required to deal with *the major points* made on a *specified topic*, the relevant material occurring *in various places throughout* the passage.

Some selective summary tasks are straightforward. For example: 'Explain in your own words the arguments advanced in favour of compulsory voting in paragraph three.'

But when, as often happens, the topic to be summarised crops up here and there throughout the passage you really do have to keep your wits about you.

Quite often, the topic specified for summarising is divided between various speakers, or treated from different points of view, or spread over more than one of several short passages that, together, constitute the material on which the summary is to be based.

In short, the material set for selective summary takes different forms, and the instructions are based on a variety of meaning. It is not possible to anticipate which of many variants you will be faced with in the examination, but if you have a thorough grasp of the summarising techniques taught in this chapter, and if you *study carefully* the *particular instructions* that you find on your paper, you need not fear this kind of question.

Test 14

No answers are provided. Exchange summaries with a fellow student. You will learn a lot by discussing each other's summaries.

Read the following letters and then carry out the instructions that follow. The letters were written for publication in a local newspaper, the second following the first a week later. Addresses have been omitted to save space.

1

Sir

Last week's meeting of the Borough Council, as reported in your issue of 6 July, showed clearly that most of our elected representatives are unable to distinguish between the real and the supposed needs of the people of this town.

I refer to the two astonishing decisions taken: to take no action on the Youth Committee's recommendation that the Youth Club premises should be enlarged and modernised; and to proceed immediately with the scheme to provide 'adequate facilities in the Borough Hall for the entertainment of distinguished visitors and for civic functions'.

Speakers in the debates emphasised the need to economise and pointed out that the plans for the Youth Club would cost more than double those for the Borough Hall. They seemed oblivious of the fact that the more expensive scheme would benefit everybody in Millport, whereas the £10,000 to be spent on the Borough Hall would achieve no practical results whatever.

We have all been disturbed by the growing evidence that some of the young people of Millport have little sense of responsibility for or loyalty to the community. Extreme examples of this disaffection are provided by cases coming before the Courts. More worrying is the widespread feeling among them - voiced freely to adults who have their confidence - that the town does little for, and has no interest in, its youngsters. Those of us who have bothered to take an interest in the present dingy and ill-equipped Youth Club premises cannot dismiss this as an altogether unfounded belief.

I would be the last to argue that adequate recreational facilities would solve all our teenage problems in this town. That they would, however, be of immense help and encouragement to all those who are concerned in training youth to use leisure wisely and creatively - and what responsible citizen is not? - is, I should have thought, obvious.

It is, perhaps, not too late to persuade the Borough Council to reconsider these two decisions. I appeal particularly to Councillor Portreve - prominent in his opposition to the Youth Club scheme - who, together with all other members of the party that he leads in the

Council, stressed in a joint election address that he would do everything in his power 'to further plans for the education and benefit of young people'. I feel sure that he and his followers cannot have forgotten so soon the pledges that they made during their election campaigns.

Yours faithfully
John Smith

2

Sir

It is a well-known fact that public men must expect abuse and ingratitude. Those of us who give our time freely to civic affairs do not expect thanks, but we have a right to justice. I refer to Mr Smith's attack upon me and those whom I have the honour to lead in the Millport Borough Council. His letter, published in your correspondence columns last week, cries out to be answered.

Citizens of Millport who have some concern for the dignity and reputation of the town - and despite Mr Smith, these are, I am happy to say, to be numbered in their thousands - have long been perturbed by the fact that the facilities at the Borough Hall for welcoming and entertaining our civic guests are woefully inadequate. There are those, I know - and Mr Smith is doubtless of that ilk - who equate courtesy with extravagance, hospitality with indulgence, and harmless wining and dining with the Seven Deadly Sins. But I am persuaded that such Killjoys are in minority and that most of my fellow Millportians take a more liberal and gracious view of life.

Let me tell Mr Smith, and any other misguided person who happens to share his narrow notions, that a trifle spent on beautifying and dignifying the Borough Hall will be far from wasted. Visitors made to feel welcome, refreshed in mind and body, will take away golden opinions of this old town of ours. They will spread our reputation and this will be reflected in increased trade and prosperity. 'Cast your bread upon the waters', we are told. In an age when - economically speaking - we have our backs to the wall, cheeseparing will not do.

It is too much to expect that Mr Smith, with his spendthrift policies, has ever heard of that inexorable law of economics: the law of diminishing returns. But I and those who are of my political persuasion have that law ever before our eyes and engraved in letters of fire, in the forefront of our minds. Let me put it in simple words for Mr Smith: 'You Can't Have Your Cake And Eat It.' He carefully refrained from mentioning what his pet scheme would cost - £25,000. Think of that, Mr Smith. Twenty-five thousand pounds - *of ratepayers' money*. People are often very generous with other people's money, but I and my supporters are, as we always have been, watchdogs over the civic coffers. Wise investment is one thing: the slippery slope to the Slough of Despond is another.

Finally, Sir, let me trespass upon the hospitality of your columns a further space and assure all those who did me the honour of electing me to the Borough Council that I will defend the reputation and dignity of Millport with my last breath. Nothing that Mr Smith can say, no pistol that he holds to my head, will make me change my views or my chosen course one iota. When money needs to be spent I will vote for its spending, albeit in doing so I may lose the support of Mr Smith and such friends as he may happen to possess. When money is proposed to be wasted I will vote against such spendthrift measures, though my principles may cost me dear and lose me a popularity I never sought. The approbation of a clear conscience and the adornment of our civic life will prove ample compensation for a vacated chair in the council chamber.

I have the honour to be, Sir,
Your obedient servant
H. Probyn Portreve

1 Explain in not more than 10 of your own words Mr Smith's reasons for objecting to the expenditure on the Borough Hall.

2 What arguments does Councillor Portreve advance to refute Mr Smith's objections? Answer in not more than 15 of your own words.

3 Give in your own words a résumé of Mr Smith's argument that the Youth Club scheme would be of benefit to Milltown as a whole. (Your answer should be about 25 words in length.)

4 Express in not more than 10 of your own words Councillor Portreve's objections to the plan for the Youth Club.

5 Express the gist of Councillor Portreve's final paragraph in one short sentence, using your own words.

Note The style in which Councillor Portreve wrote may have caused you some problems when you were making summaries of material selected from his letter. (For example, he makes heavy use of figures of speech, and these have no place in summary.) Had the selective summary questions been accompanied by comprehension questions, as they might well have been in an examination paper, some of the latter would undoubtedly have been based on the councillor's use (or misuse) of language.

For a discussion of style and vocabulary see Chapter 5.

Test 15

My suggested answer is on page 171. Do not turn to it before working out your own answer.

Read this passage carefully. Then make a plan for a précis of the passage. Use your own words when making the plan and remember to head your plan with a brief statement of the gist of the passage. (Revise 4.4(f) and 4.4 (i) before starting work.)

Perhaps it has never struck you that scientific inventions can be very helpful to the artist? Then the following story may be of interest. The horse has always been a favourite subject but have you ever realised that it was not until the closing years of the nineteenth century that a galloping horse could be truthfully depicted? The reason is that the human eye is not quick enough to observe accurately the movements of a horse's legs when in rapid motion. The consequence was that, until the invention of slow-motion films, no artist had any idea what a galloping horse really did with its legs. So, for centuries, the moving horse was painted, either rearing up on its hind legs and pawing the air with its front hooves (which, of course, it may do, but not when galloping), or in the celebrated 'flying gallop', its front legs extended forward and its hind legs extended backwards. This flying gallop posture was suggestive of great speed and was very successful artistically, though a little thought will show that a horse in such a position would be an anatomical impossibility. The convention lasted, however, until slow-motion pictures enabled artists to achieve realism without loss of movement in their studies of galloping horses.

4.6 DIRECT AND INDIRECT (REPORTED) SPEECH

The rules for the correct punctuation of direct speech are set out in Chapter 8, but it is necessary to deal with indirect speech in this chapter on Summary. For this reason:

● All *direct speech* in the original passage *must be changed into indirect speech* in the summary.

(a) Definitions
Direct speech is a *direct representation* in writing of the words *actually spoken*:

John said, 'I'm late because I overslept.'

Indirect speech is a *report* in writing of the words *actually spoken*:

John said that he was late because he had overslept.

That is why *reported speech* is the alternative name for 'indirect speech'.

(b) The use of reported speech in summary

It used to be obligatory to write all précis in reported speech. The précis writer was expected to begin his précis with a 'formula' introduction such as this:

> *The writer states that* there were three reasons for the decline of rural transport in the mid-twentieth century.

Examiners no longer insist on this. Nowadays you are encouraged to express the writer's material directly, as if it were your own – provided, of course, that you do not copy out the writer's actual words. So, the accepted presentation of the above is:

> There were three reasons for the decline of rural transport in the mid-twentieth century.

However, the use of reported speech is still compulsory in the following circumstances:

(i) When the examiner's instructions say, 'Make a précis of the following passage in reported speech.' Examiners do, from time to time, insist on this. They are perfectly entitled to do so. Candidates are expected to be capable of using reported speech *and* they are expected to read the instructions.

(ii) Whenever direct speech occurs in the original passage, and you need to include that material in your summary because it is a key point, you *must* change it into reported speech. You must never quote in a summary.

Suppose that the following seems to you to embody a key point in the passage that you are summarising:

> 'I'm perfectly certain', said Councillor Jones, 'that the ratepayers will get steamed up about this proposal.'

The remark must be *reported* in your summary, like this:

> Councillor Jones said that he was convinced that the ratepayers would be angry about that proposal.

Notes on the above example

1 'perfectly certain' becomes 'convinced'. The précis-writer is using his own words and condensing.

2 'I'm' becomes 'he was'.

3 'will' becomes 'would be'

4 'steamed up' becomes 'angry'. The style of a summary is always formal. Figures of speech are not used.

Those notes draw attention to some of the rules for the writing of reported spech. These are discussed now.

(c) The rules of reported speech

(i) A 'saying' verb followed by 'that' introduces reported speech, as in the example given earlier:

'John said that he was late because he had overslept.' The 'saying' verb is not always 'said'. It can be an 'expressive' saying verb, useful to the summariser because it conveys swiftly and economically the tone or purpose of the speech that is being reported:

The prisoner protested that he had been denied access to his solicitor. Robinson objected that the item had not been discussed in committee.

(ii) The tense of the 'saying' verb governs the tenses of all the verbs used in the reported speech. This, if you look at it realistically, is just a matter of common sense. You cannot put your meaning across if you jumble up the tenses. These examples illustrate tense rules:

The 'saying' verb is often in the past tense. When it is, the verbs in the reported speech must be in the past tense, too:

The chairman reported that his committee had given the fullest consideration to that point but announced that it had felt unable to change its recommendation.

If, however, the 'saying' verb is in the present tense, then the tenses of the verbs in the reported speech are adjusted accordingly; like this:

Our special correspondent writes that conditions in the devastated area are improving slowly and that it should be possible to restore railway communications fairly soon.

(iii) When direct speech is turned into reported speech all pronouns and possessive adjectives must be changed into the *third person*. For example:

Direct speech   The rebel leader announced his acceptance of the terms of the truce, saying: 'It shall never be asserted that I prolonged this struggle unnecessarily. The lives of my men are precious to me, and our cause has always been that of the people of our country.'

Indirect (reported) speech   The rebel leader announced his acceptance of the terms of the truce and declared that it should never be asserted that he had prolonged that struggle unnecessarily. The lives of his men were precious to him, and their cause had always been that of the people of their country.

(iv) The necessity of using only third-person pronouns and possessive adjectives can give rise to ambiguity - a fatal weakness in any writing, and especially in summary. A competent summariser avoids this fault by substituting appropriate nouns for pronouns and possessive nouns for possessive adjectives. Here is an example of how it can be done:

Ambiguous   He said that he had followed his proposals carefully and his objections to them would be quite clear to them when they had heard what he had to say in his speech.

Improved   He said that he had followed the last speaker's proposals carefully and his objections to them would be quite clear to the members of the audience when they had heard what he had to say in his own speech.

(v) Adjectives and adverbs indicating nearness in place and in time in direct speech are changed in reported speech into adjectives and adverbs expressive of a 'distancing' effect. For example, 'this' becomes 'that'; 'today' becomes 'that day'. Like the tenses, these adjectives and adverbs 'go back one', so to speak – as in this passage:

Direct speech   The delegate said: 'My union sent me here to find a solution to this long-standing problem. We have set ourselves a time limit for the conclusion of this troublesome business, but we are prepared to be patient until it becomes clear to us that the will to succeed does not exist on your side. We want an agreement by the end of next month.'

Reported speech   The delegate said that his union had sent him there to find a solution to that long-standing problem. They had set themselves a time limit for the conclusion of that troublesome business, but they were prepared to be patient until it became clear to them that the will to succeed did not exist on the other side. They wanted an agreement by the end of the following month.

(vi) Colloquialisms and contractions are not used in reported speech.

Direct speech (extract from a letter)   'I'd better tell you that I've decided not to be your candidate at the next election – whenever it comes – and I'll probably get it off my chest at the committee meeting next Jan.'

Reported speech   The writer informed his correspondent that he had decided not to be their candidate at the election, whenever that occurred, and that he would take an early opportunity of announcing that decision. He would probably do so at the committee meeting in the following January.

As the above example shows, slang is not used in reported speech, either.

Test 16
Answer on page 171.
Rewrite the following passage in reported speech.

The chief opposition spokesman for education said: 'I have listened to the minister's speech with care but I find nothing new or constructive in his proposals. Indeed, I regard his speech as a flagrant betrayal of his party's election promises. Far from spending more on education, he proposes to hold expenditure at this year's level. In a time of rising prices that is tantamount to reducing the money spent on education, and I accuse him of weakening the service that it is his duty to strengthen.'

CHAPTER 5

USING (AND MISUSING) WORDS

5.1 VOCABULARY

(a) Definition
The *Shorter Oxford English Dictionary* supplies several definitions of the word 'vocabulary'. The one that I have chosen to use here fits the sense in which the word will be used in this section: 'The range of language of a particular person . . .'

(b) The advantages of a large vocabulary
Your vocabulary is the range of words that you can use. The larger it is, the better will be your performance in all aspects of English-language work. A large vocabulary helps you to express your ideas precisely, vividly, and without repeating yourself in *composition*. You cannot do well in *comprehension* without a large vocabulary, for the passages and questions involve a range of words much wider than that of daily conversation. When *summarising*, the need to condense makes it essential that you have an ample stock of words from which to make an apt selection.

All your other subjects will also benefit if your vocabulary is large; and a good command of words adds greatly to your capacity to deal successfully with the worlds of work and leisure that lie outside and beyond the life of school and the examination room.

5.2 DIFFERENT VOCABULARIES

(a) The wealth of words
The English language is rich in its enormous range of words, having been for centuries an 'importer' of words from other languages; words which it then anglicised and used as if they were 'native'.

Another source of this wealth of words was the fusion that took place (over a long period) between the Anglo-Saxon (or 'Old English') language of the English – itself already enriched by Celtic and Latin words – and the Norman-French language of the conquerors of 1066. This fusion resulted in profound changes in vocabulary and, of course, in grammar.

I have not the space to do more than mention the fascinating story of our English tongue, but I do recommend you to learn about it. A knowledge of its history helps you to use the English language with greater confidence and fluency. Two excellent (and quite short) books on the subject are: Otto Jespersen's *Growth and Structure of the English Language* and Henry Bradley's *The Making of English*.

Centuries of word formation and importation and language blending have resulted in a larger stock of words than is possessed by any other language. The *Oxford English Dictionary* lists about half a million words.

Not even highly educated people have more than a small fraction of this huge total of words at their command. Outstanding linguists may have a vocabulary of, perhaps, 25,000 or 30,000 words. An 'average educated' vocabulary is estimated at 12,000 to 15,000 words. You can get by in everyday English – used merely for the commonplace activities of life – with about 2500 words.

Those numbers are approximate and they are not put forward as 'targets'. Your job – for the reasons stated earlier – is steadily to build up your stock of usable words.

(b) Listening and speaking; reading and writing

We all have four different vocabularies, used in those four separate communication activities.

Of the words that we hear, we understand some that we are not confident enough to use in our own speech.

Of the words that we read, we understand some that we are not confident enough to use in our own writing.

Our listening vocabulary is larger than our speaking vocabulary. Our reading vocabulary is larger than our writing vocabulary.

Another way of putting it is this: we all have a passive vocabulary and an active vocabulary. By taking an interest in words (noticing them and thinking about their meaning and their use) we can enlarge both. The ideal is constantly to narrow the gap between our active vocabulary and an ever-growing passive vocabulary.

(c) Specialised and general

This chapter began with a definition of the word 'vocabulary'. The quotation from the dictionary was left incomplete. In full, the definition reads: 'The range of language of a particular person, class, profession'.

The English language has a vocabulary of half a million words. An individual has a vocabulary drawn from the total number of words theoretically available to him from that huge store and then applied to the situations in which he finds himself in the various activities of his life. That is his vocabulary – his *general* vocabulary.

The individual may also have a *specialised* vocabulary, arising from particular circumstances of his life and work. An electrician, a nuclear physicist, a joiner, a doctor, a plumber, an airline pilot . . . all these, and many more, have to have specialised vocabularies in order to be able to do their jobs.

Lawyers, journalists, politicians, actors, printers, publishers . . . all have specialised vocabularies. So do cricketers, pupils at a particular school, football fans, pop-music addicts, Cockneys, Yorkshire men and women, people who live in Devon or Cornwall, or Lancashire, or Somerset, or . . .

When the specialised vocabulary arises from a geographical circumstance we call it a *dialect* vocabulary, but it is a specialised vocabulary, just as an *occupational* or *leisure interest* vocabulary is a specialised vocabulary.

Sometimes expressions belonging to a specialised vocabulary enter the general vocabulary of the language. For example, 'getting into the charts' is now used generally to describe the achievement of popularity. It has nothing to do with navigation; it originated in the vocabulary of the pop-music world.

No doubt you can think of many other examples of words that were once specialised but are now in the general vocabulary. (Have a look at Brewer's *Dictionary of Phrase and Fable* and Eric Partridge's *Dictionary of Cliché*. Both books should be in your school or college library.)

With such exceptions, however, the words of a specialised vocabulary, useful as they are, should be used only in the specialised contexts in which they have a precise meaning. The use of items from a specialised vocabulary in an inappropriate context is a fault. See Section 5.6.

5.3 VOCABULARY-BUILDING

Earlier, you were encouraged to take an interest in words. It hardly needs saying that you cannot build your vocabulary unless you become interested in words. You would not expect to become proficient in playing a musical instrument or a game in which you had no interest. You cannot expect to enlarge your vocabulary unless you take a lively interest in the words that you hear and read and in the words that you speak and write.

'Taking an interest in' words means doing something about them. A genuine interest leads to activity.

First, you must *notice* words. You must 'prick your ears up' when you hear a word that you have not heard before or – just as important – when you hear a word used in a way that you have not heard it used before. You must 'open your eyes' when you read a word that you have not seen written before or – again – used in a way that you have not seen it used before.

Then, having trained yourself to notice words, you have follow-up work to do. Most importantly, you must get into the habit of using your dictionary.

(a) Dictionaries

There are three kinds of dictionaries:

(i) 'Desk' dictionaries. One-volume, 'short' dictionaries, admirably suited to your present needs.

(ii) 'Library' dictionaries. Multi-volume works of reference, providing exhaustive information about words – their meanings, their derivations (etymologies), their use in the past and their use nowadays. The most famous is the *Oxford English Dictionary* – the world-renowned *O.E.D.*

(iii) Specialist dictionaries. Devoted to the vocabulary of various specialised subjects. There are dictionaries of science, history, psychology, economics, geography, sports and pastimes, slang, clichés, proverbs, quotations, etc.

In this book we shall concentrate on desk dictionaries, since that is the kind that you own and must learn how to use.

(b) How to use your dictionary

Even though a desk dictionary contains fewer words than a library dictionary, it still contains a lot. There are 1444 pages in the body of the third edition of the *Concise Oxford Dictionary*, taking the reader from **A** to **zymotic**, plus 61 pages of addenda, consisting 'of (1) words not recorded in the body of the dictionary, and (2) further senses and constructions of words already treated'.

Because the lexicographer (dictionary-maker or -compiler) is cramming a great deal of information into one book he has to use abbreviations and a fairly complicated and rigidly observed system of 'code signals', such as different type faces and brackets of various kinds.

To put your dictionary to good use you must familiarise yourself with the lexicographer's abbreviations, his symbols and his pronunciation signs. Not all dictionaries use identical 'codes' so you must get to know those that are used in yours.

Here is the *Concise Oxford*'s entry for the word we are now discussing:

di.ctionary, n. Book dealing, usu. in alphabetical order, with the words of a language or of some special subject, author, &c., wordbook, lexicon (*French-English* &c., *d*., of French &c. words with English &c. explanation; *d. of architecture* or *the Bible, Shakespeare d*., &c.); *walking* or *living d*., well-informed person; *d. English, style*, &c., over-correct, pedantic. [f. med. L *dictionarium* (prec., −ARY[1])]

The lexicographer has tried to supply in that entry all the information about the word 'dictionary' that you are likely to need. He has also shown you some of the ways - those in most common use - in which you can employ it.

The list of abbreviations and other 'code signals' at the beginning of the *Concise Oxford Dictionary of Current English* (to give the book its full title) explains all the information given in the entry. If you know the code you can 'translate' the entry.

1 The word is pronounced with the stress on the first syllable ('di.ction-ary').

2 It is a noun ('n').

3 Its definition follows, and we learn from it that the words in a dic-tionary are usually ('usu.') arranged in alphabetical order. We also learn that a dictionary is either general ('the words of a language') or specialised ('of some special subject, author, &c.').

4 A dictionary is a 'wordbook' or 'lexicon'.

5 Examples of wordbooks or lexicons given: French-English Dictionary, containing French words with English explanations; and the '&c.' tells us that there are similar dictionaries of other languages; for example, a German–Spanish Dictionary would contain German words with Spanish explanations.

6 Examples of specialist dictionaries are: a dictionary of architecture, a dictionary of the Bible, a Shakespeare dictionary, etc.

7 We also learn that the word can be used figuratively (see Section 5.5). We can refer to somebody as a 'walking dictionary' or a 'living dictionary', meaning that he is well-informed. We can refer to some-body's use of English as 'dictionary English' or to his writing as 'dictionary style', meaning that his way of talking or writing is over-correct or pedantic.

8 Finally, we learn that the word is derived from a medieval Latin word - *dictionarium*. For further information about its derivation we are referred to the preceding word in the dictionary ('prec.,'). That word is *diction* which, the dictionary tells us, came into English from the Latin word *dictio*, which was itself derived from *dicere*, meaning 'say'.

You will not always need to squeeze every drop of information out of an entry; but you will *always* need: (1) to learn the pronunciation and spelling of the word; (2) to study the definitions; (3) to select from the definitions the particular sense (and usage) applicable to the context in which the word is being used or to the context in which you want to use the word.

Test 17
You will find the answer in your dictionary.
The words in a dictionary are arranged in *strict* alphabetical order. So, *dictate* precedes *dictator*, which precedes *dictatorial*, which precedes *diction*. Write out the following words in the order in which they would appear in a dictionary.

equator	equatorial	equilateral
equate	equalise	equip
equal	equality	equine
equally	equinox	equilibrium

Test 18
Answer on page 171.
On each page of the dictionary that I am using two words are printed in bold type at the head. For example, on page 639 'largely' and 'last' appear at the top. Examine your own dictionary. Now explain what the two words tell you about the contents of page 639 in my dictionary.

(c) Notes on meaning
You are familiar with the instruction in comprehension questions to explain the meaning of a word *in the sense in which it is used* in the passage. And, earlier in this chapter, we saw that 'dictionary' and 'vocabulary' have more than one meaning. It is vital to remember that most words do.

- Multiple meanings are common. The particular meaning of a word depends upon the context in which it is being used.

So, when you are using your dictionary you must be very careful to select the meaning appropriate to the context in which you have found the word that you are looking up. You must be equally careful to ascertain that the word you are looking up can have the meaning that you wish it to convey in the context in which you are intending to use it.

We shall return to the subject of meaning and context, but here is an example to show how complicated a 'simple' word can be.

In my dictionary I find that the word 'flock' can be used either as a noun or as a verb. As a noun it can be used to signify: a lock, tuft, of wool, cotton, etc.; material used for quilting and stuffing made from waste wool or torn-up cloth; powdered wool or cloth for paper-making; a light, loose particle precipitated during chemical or cooking processes; a large number of people; a number of animals of one kind, especially birds, feeding or travelling together; a number of domestic animals, usually sheep, goats, or geese kept together; the Christian body; a congregation, especially in relation to its pastor; a family of children; a number of pupils. As a verb it can describe the action of forming flocks, as in chemistry or cookery; the action of going about together in great numbers; the action of preparing wool, cotton material, etc., to make flock.

Your dictionary cannot tell you which of a word's potential meanings you need. It gives you as many meanings as it has space for, and it suggests some of the commonest ways in which the word is used. It is up to you to select the meaning and usage appropriate to your purposes.

(d) Notes on pronunciation

The best way of learning the 'code' supplied in your dictionary is to apply it to each word as you look it up. If you work out the pronunciation by referring from the word to the code you will soon know how the code works. It is a lengthy and usually pointless process to start by trying to learn the code by heart.

Nor should you suppose that the lexicographer lays down the law. He records the way (or ways) in which words are usually pronounced.

So, if you look up *pedagogy* your dictionary will tell you that the stress (or 'accent', as it is also called) falls on the first syllable; that the three vowels are short; that the first *g* is hard; that the second *g* is *either* hard *or* soft ('-gi, -ji'); and that the *y* is pronounced like a short *i*.

Whatever particular symbols the 'pronunciation code' in your dictionary employs it directs your attention to:

1 the pronunciation of the vowels;

2 the pronunciation of the consonants;

3 the pronunciation of consonant pairs (such as rough/bough);

4 special difficulties of pronunciation (such as archangel -*k*-, but archbishop; orchard -*tsh*-, but orchestra -*k*-);

5 the position of the stress or accent.

(e) Notes on spelling

What your dictionary does is to record the accepted spelling; and it may draw your attention to accepted alternative spellings. Sometimes, you will find in the preface that a whole series of alternative spellings has been dealt with in a blanket note such as this (from the *Concise Oxford*): '. . . verbs that contain the suffix *-ize* . . . are all given without the alternative forms in *-ise*, although these are still the commoner in British (as opposed to American) printing.' The note tells us, in other words, that we can spell *specialise* either *-ise* or *-ize*.

It is important to be consistent. The publishers of this book, for example, point out to their authors that 'the copy-editor will usually apply certain conventions for the sake of consistency', and instance the following: '-*ise* spellings (e.g. organise, organisation) in all cases where *s* and *z* are alternatives.'

Use *judgement* or *judgment*, but stick to your chosen alternative. It is not sensible to jolt your reader's attention away from the content of your writing by presenting him with *judgement* in one place and *judgment* in another. (The latter form is habitually used in legal works.)

If you follow your dictionary's spelling you will know that you are right. You cannot always be sure that somebody else's spelling is wrong - not until you have studied all that your dictionary tells you about the spelling(s) that it uses and the way(s) in which it deals with accepted alternatives.

(f) Making a wordbook of your own

If you try to do this as a duty - a painstaking attempt to enlarge your vocabulary - that will be laudable, but you will not keep it up for long. It is too laborious a task unless you bring a collector's zest to it.

If you can collect words, as a keen train- or plane-spotter collects trains or planes, you will equip yourself with a most valuable tool, the use of which will do wonders for your word-power.

A small notebook that you can carry around is ideal. Allow plenty of space for each word - a page for each is not too much. Jot down any word that you hear or see each day that attracts your attention because: (i) it is new to you; (ii) it is not new to you *but* you have never heard/seen it used in that way before; (iii) it makes a pleasant noise; (iv) it makes a horrible noise; (v) it strikes you as being perfectly, uniquely, *right* for the purpose for which it is being used; (vi) it is funny; (vii) it is sad; (viii) any other reason that seems good to you.

As soon as possible, look it up in your dictionary. Note the meaning that it had in the context in which you heard/saw it. If you think that it was a misuse of the word, note that. Note any interesting points about its history - where did it come from? - has it changed its meaning as it got older? Note any points that interest you in relation to the occasion on which it was used and the purpose for which it was used. Check on its subsequent uses when it appears again in your growing lingustic experience.

A wordbook can be the basis of an absorbing, lifelong hobby, and a very profitable one.

The final advice must be: read widely and listen attentively. Good readers and listeners usually become good writers and speakers.

5.4 WORD FORMATION

(a) Syllables

You learnt early on in your study of English that your spelling improves if you pay attention to the syllables that form words. For example, it is easy to spell cup/board if you think of its two syllables; and you will not mis-spell im/me/di/ate/ly if you break it up into its five syllables.

Improved spelling is not the only advantage. Study of the syllabic for-mation of words makes it easier to grasp their meaning. In this way you add rapidly to your vocabulary and learn to make apt use of your growing word-power.

(b) Prefixes and suffixes

There is no mystery about this topic. We use words containing prefixes and suffixes every day of our lives - we have to. If a friend spoke this sentence to you it would not seem remarkable: 'It's nonsense to expect justice in a dictatorship.' Use your dictionary to help you to identify the prefixes and suffixes in those words, and you may be surprised to see how many there are.

Again, it is unlikely that there are any words in the following list that are not already part of your vocabulary: abject; inject; object; project; reject. But you may not have realised that, although each word means something different, they all *stem from* a common (Latin) *root*. It is the different prefixes (*ab-*; *in-*; *ob-*; *pro-*; *re-*) that give the words their different meanings. Use your dictionary to discover the meaning of their common element (*-ject-*).

You already know that many English words form their opposites by adding a prefix (able/*un*able; possible/*im*possible) and you know that many English adverbs are formed by adding the suffix *-ly* to the adjective.

It is not difficult to familiarise yourself with the meaning of the common prefixes and suffixes used in English. Indeed, competent performance demands that you know their meanings - that you can distinguish between, say, *ante-* and *anti-*.

The best way of learning what prefixes and suffixes mean is to pay care-ful attention to the separate elements of each words that you look up in your dictionary.

The list of prefixes and suffixes printed at the end of this section (pp. 107-8) will give you a useful start, but before using it you must remember two things.

First, remember that the list is merely a selection of the prefixes and suffixes that you will encounter. I have drawn your attention only to the commonest examples. (I have indicated the various languages from which the prefixes and suffixes come, not because you necessarily need to remember their origins, but as an interesting illustration of the point made earlier about 'imports' and 'blendings'.)

Second, remember that a prefix often changes its spelling when it is joined to a stem. For example, the (Latin) prefix *in-* means 'not'. So, when it is joined to *distinct*, we have the word *indistinct*, meaning 'not distinct'. Similarly, we join *in-* to *legal* to make a word meaning 'not legal'; but there is no such word as *inlegal* in English. The word we use is *illegal* (*in-* + *legal* = 'illegal').

This often happens. The spelling of the prefix is changed to bring about a more comfortable grafting of the prefix on to the stem.

When the spelling of the prefix is thus changed ('by assimilation') we get a double consonant at the join (the 'graft') between the prefix and the stem. This is a point to look out for in spelling (see Chapter 8).

The word *assimilation* is itself and example of 'assimilation'! It means 'being made like' or 'being absorbed into'. This is how it is formed:

stem: 'similis' (from a Latin root, meaning 'like')
prefix: 'ad-'   (Latin prefix, meaning 'to')
suffix: '-ation'   (Latin suffix, indicating abstract noun)

But when the word is formed out of these elements the *d* of *ad-* is 'made like' the first letter (*s*) of *similis*. The prefix is assimilated into the stem, and so we have 'assimilate' (*not* 'adsimilate').

PREFIXES

1   English

a-   on
aboard; ashore
be-   by, on, around, on all sides (used in many ways)
bestride; befriend; belabour; behead; beside
for-   away
forgive; forbid; forget
fore-   before (of place or time)
foreleg; foretell; forerunner
mis-   wrong
mistake; misdeed; mishap
un-   not, reverse
unripe; undo; unwind
with   against, back
withstand; withdraw

2   Latin

a-, ab-, abs-   away from

avert; absolve; abstract
ad-   to
adhere; accede; admit; adverb; aggregate
am-, amb-, ambi-   round about, both
ambidextrous; ambiguous
ante-   before
antecedent; antechamber; anticipate
bi-, bis-   twice, two
bicycle; biscuit; bilateral
circu-, circum-   round about
circumscribe; circuit; circumnagivate
co-, con-   with
concoct; conform; collect; correspond
contra-   against
contradict; controvert; countersign
cum-   with
commiserate; concoct, cohere; co-eternal

ex-, *e-*, *ef-*   from, out of
elect; extract; efflux; eject
extra-   beyond
extravagant; extraneous; extraordinary
in-   not, in
invade; impose; ineligible; impossible; irregular
non-   not
nonsense; nonentity; nonplus
ob-   in the way of, towards,
 against, in front
obstruct; occur; offer; oppose
post-   after
postpone; postdate; postwar
pre-   before
predict; prefer
re-   again, against, away, back
rejoin; rebel; remove; retrace
retro-   backwards
retrospect, retrograde
sub-   under
submit; succumb; suffer; suspend
super-, *supra-*   over, above
supernumary; superpose; superfluous
trans-   across
transatlantic; translate; traverse
vice-   instead of
viceroy; vice-chairman

3   Greek

a-, *an-*   not
atheism; anarchy; atom
anti-   against
anticlimax; antidote; antipathy
auto-   self
autograph; autobiography; authen-
 tic; automobile
mono-   single
monograph; monarchy; mono-
 theism; monoplane

pan-, *panto-*   all
panacea; panorama; pantomime
para-   beside, as, beyond
parable; parody; paramilitary
peri-   around, about
perimeter; periphrasis
poly-   many
polysyllabic; polyglot; polytechnic
syn-   together, with
syntax; system; syllable; symbol;
 sympathy
tele-   far
telephone; television; telepathy

SUFFIXES

Denoting abstract nouns   English:
man*hood*; God*head*; wis*dom*;
dark*ness*; hat*red*; steward*ship*.
Latin: was*tage*; priva*cy*; prud*ence*;
just*ice*; cult*ure*. Greek: sarc*asm*;
hero*ism*; monarch*y*
Denoting agent or doer   English:
fath*er*; coster*monger*; pok*er*; shov*el*.
Latin: occup*ant*; antiqu*ary*; vic*ar*;
chancell*or*; ward*en*. Greek: man*iac*;
crit*ic*; roy*alist*
Adjective suffixes   English:
feather*ed*; wood*en*; leath*ern*;
mani*fold*; merci*ful*; fiend*ish*;
penni*less*; child*like*; friend*ly*;
end*most*; loath*some*; wind*y*.
Latin: aud*acious*; ment*al*; hum*an*;
cert*ain*; hum*ane*; err*ant*; provid*ent*;
angul*ar*; desol*ate*; host*ile*; flex*ible*;
pens*ive*; peril*ous*. Greek: gigant*ic*;
eulog*istic*
Verb suffixes   English: glimm*er*;
spark*le*; quick*en*; hark; length*en*.
Latin: infl*ate*; coale*sce*; puri*fy*;
aboli*sh*. Greek: civil*ise*
Adverb suffix   English: loud*ly*

(c) Word-borrowing and word-coining

A living language is changing all the time. The way we use English words
in phrases and in sentences (the grammar of the language) has evolved
over centuries and it is still changing (see Chapter 6). Changes in vocabulary have been equally remarkable.

Growth has come from literary influences (words from Latin, Greek, and the modern European languages); from war (especially Dutch, German, and French words); from trade (words taken from Arabic, Malay, Spanish, Turkish, and almost every spoken tongue); from word-coining to express new ideas, especially in science, philosophy, and psychology (such coined words are often based on foreign roots to which are added Greek, Latin, French, or German prefixes and/or suffixes).

Again, words change their meaning and the ways in which they are used. In the seventeenth century *conceit* had a different meaning from the one we give it today. Shakespeare could use *fool* as a term of endearment as well as in disparagement; and *naughty* meant 'worthless. and 'wicked'. For centuries *bloody* was not 'impolite'. Words go up and down the social scale and the scale of formality. They come into and go out of fashion.

The chief sources of vocabulary growth and word formation are:

(i) By the addition of prefixes and suffixes to a stem. See Section 5.4 (b).

(ii) By direct 'importation' from other languages. For example: *Dutch* - spool, trek, skipper; *Arabic* –coffee (*via* Turkish), algebra; *German* –waltz, swindle; *Hebrew* - jubilee, amen; *Italian* - sonnet, stanza; *Persian* - bazaar (*via* Turkish and Italian), caravan; *Russian* - bolshevik, steppe; *Spanish* - armada, banana.

(iii) By joining two or more words together (with or without a hyphen). For example: looking-glass, outlaw, God-fearing, nationwide, underwrite. (See Chapter 8, where the use of the hyphen is discussed.)

(iv) By the invention or coining of words for special purposes, usually to describe inventions or new scientific developments or fields of study. For example: *geology* was coined from two Greek words, *gē*(earth) and *logos* (discourse); *psychology* was coined from the Greek word *psukhē* (soul or mind) plus *logos*; *bicycle* was coined from the Latin prefix *bi-* (twice or two) and the Greek root *kuklos* (wheel); *television* was coined from the Greek prefix *tele-* (far) and the Latin root *videre* (to see). When coined words contain elements from more than one language, they are called 'hybrids'.

(v) By derivation from proper names, either in English or in foreign languages. For example: *academy* comes from the Greek name for the garden near Athens in which Plato taught; *boycott* comes from the name of a certain Captain Boycott, an Irish landlord who was ostracised by his neighbours in 1880.

I hope that you will follow up this fascinating subject of vocabulary growth and word formation. Find out all that you can about the words you use. There are many books about words and the English language. I recommend as a starter *Our Language* by Simeon Potter (Penguin), especially chapter VII, 'Word Creation'.

5.5 SYNONYMS, ANTONYMS, AND HOMOPHONES

It is useful to study the meaning of these terms before tackling the kind of vocabulary and word usage tests that are involved in examinations. A knowledge of synonyms, especially, suggests approaches to language that add to your understanding of how words work.

(a) Synonyms

The word 'synonym' comes from Greek (*syn* plus *onoma*) and it means 'with the same name'. Synonyms are words that mean the same thing, or very nearly the same thing. (Examples are: leap/jump; slay/kill; start/begin.) For the reasons set out earlier in this chapter the English language is rich in synonyms.

However, synonyms are *not* instantly interchangeable words. Whenever you want to substitute one word for another, as you often do in composition, comprehension, or summary, you have to decide whether the word that you are considering as a substitute carries the particular *shade* of meaning that you require.

Your choice involves the following considerations:

1 Words arouse and convey feelings as well as ideas (see Section 5.6). So, for example, although *slay* 'means' *kill* (and *kill* 'means' *slay*) no competent writer would substitute 'slain' for 'killed' in this newspaper headline: 'Fifteen Killed on County's Roads in Bank Holiday Black Week.'

2 Very rarely do two words mean exactly the same thing, though they may mean something very similar. For example, although *start* and *begin* can 'mean the same' you would choose 'started' rather than 'began' to fill the gap in this sentence: 'The mayor — the 3.30 race at Sandwood, run over two and a half miles for the newly presented Borough Trophy.'

3 Words must be appropriate to the context in which they are used. The context is not merely the sentence in which the words occurs but the whole of the paragraph of which that sentence forms a part. Indeed, the *passage*, as a whole, must be taken into account when a choice of words is being made. For example, although *buy* 'means' *purchase* and *live* 'means' *reside*, you cannot just shuffle them around and slot one in instead of the other. There are contexts in which 'purchase' and 'reside' would be the wrong choices. They are *not* simple alternatives for 'buy' and 'live'. (See Section 5.6.)

4 Words have sounds – even written or printed words are 'heard' by a reader. The sound of the words you are using is an important consideration. No writer sensitive to the sound of his words would permit himself to write a 'jingle' such as this: 'The general generally expects his subordinates to

report their major decisions to him in writing.' (And having substituted 'usually' for 'generally', would you be happy about 'major', later in the sentence? Surely 'chief' would be better *in that context*? The point is a different one, but important.) *Euphony*, then, is to be considered when choosing words.

(b) Antonyms

The word 'antonym' also comes from Greek (*anti-* plus *onoma*) and means 'against a name'. Antonyms are words of opposite meaning: long/short; difficult/easy; known/unknown; good/bad. Many of the considerations that apply when choosing among synonyms apply also when selecting antonyms.

A long journey is (in respect of length) the opposite of a short journey, but opposites are not always quite so straightforward. These two sentences do *not* express a *simple* contrast – they are not 'black and white' opposites: 'I think this fish is good.'/'I think this fish is bad.' Think about them.

(c) Homophones

Greek again: *homos*, 'the same' plus phonē, 'sound'. Homophones are words having the same sound but different meanings. For example: gait/ gate; fare/fair; be/bee; would/wood. The identity of sound can lead to careless slips, though a little thought should keep you strait/straight in this sentence: 'You would be stopped at the ticket-collector's gate if you had not paid you railfare.'

5.6 HOW WORDS ARE USED

(a) Sense of purpose and sense of audience

Success in using words depends on having:

- a clearly-thought-out purpose;
- a clear sense of audience.

Get into the habit of asking yourself:

- *Why* am I saying/writing these words?
- *To whom* am I saying/writing these words?

If you ask (and answer) those questions your choice of words (and the order in which you use them – see Chapter 6) will improve.

For example, the practical writing question in the examination could well offer you this kind of choice:

Write a letter suitable to the circumstances described in *one* of the following:

(a) As secretary to your school current affairs society you have been instructed by the committee to write to the chairman of your local education authority asking him to speak at a meeting of your society. Write the invitation, remembering to give full details of time, place, date, and of suggested topics.

(b) You read in your local paper that the mother of a friend of yours has been awarded a degree by the Open University. Write a letter of congratulation that conveys a sense of admiration for her achievement and that shows your understanding of the hard work and determination called for by the years of study.

The two tasks have some features in common. They are practical writing exercises. They are letters written by a younger person to an older reader. They demand a knowledge of the conventions of letter-writing.

However, the differences between the two are at least as important as their similarities. Sense of purpose and sense of audience should alert the writer to the need to draw on different areas of his vocabulary according to which of the two letters he is writing.

The *purpose* of the first letter is to invite somebody to accept a speaking engagement. Such a purpose is best fulfilled by the use of crisp, clear-cut business-like language. The utmost clarity is required.

The *purpose* of the second letter is to convey the writer's feelings of shared pleasure in an achievement and his admiration of the qualities of mind and character that made the achievement possible.

The *audience* for the first letter is a stranger, occupying an important position. The writer's choice of words should reflect the degree of formality required, and – though a favour is being asked – an impersonal tone is to be maintained, appropriate to the official nature of the correspondence.

The *audience* for the second letter is well known to the writer. As the mother of the writer's friend, she has a social relationship with the writer. The language must be appropriate to a personal correspondence. The tone should be warmer than would be acceptable in the first letter.

● *Remember*, you cannot choose *appropriate* words unless you keep your mind clear about your *purpose* in using them and the *audience* for whom they are intended.

(b) Literal and figurative use of words

Everyday speech and writing provide ample proof of the frequency with which words are used figuratively. Expressions such as 'having a finger in the pie', 'over the moon', 'cooking the books' are in everyone's vocabulary.

We do not suppose that someone described as having 'cooked the books' has been boiling books in a saucepan. We all know that the expression means 'falsifying the accounts'.

Similarly, we do not interpret 'having a finger in the pie' as meaning *literally* what it says. We know that it means having a share in some action or enterprise, and that it describes an officious person, a meddler, and one who, as a rule, interferes to seek his own advantage.

Unfortunately, a sloppy-minded habit has arisen of seeking to emphasise these figurative (or metaphorical) expressions by qualifying them with the word *literally*. The following example typifies this misuse of language. A pools winner, interviewed on television, and asked how he felt when he learnt of his good fortune, answered: 'Literally, over the moon.' A nonsensical statement, of course.

The objections to this habit are not trivial. First, it is never desirable to utter nonsense. Second, the misuse of 'literal' weakens the legitimate employment of language figuratively (or metaphorically). Third, if you acquire this silly trick, you will lose marks in the examination by failing to distinguish between words and expressions used literally and those used figuratively.

The examining boards do not, as a rule, ask candidates to identify 'figures of speech' (see below), but they test their use of words in a way that makes a knowledge of the commonest 'figures' very useful; and they do expect candidates to have a clear understanding of the distinction between the literal and figurative uses of words.

An example of the type of question set will make the point clear.

Select three of the following words and use each in two sentences in which the word is (i) used literally; (ii) metaphorically: sweets; straw; knot; golden; pastures.

Example: leaden

(i) The outer shell of oak, reinforced by a leaden lining, had preserved the contents of the coffer through three centuries of exposure to the elements. (literal)

(ii) My enduring memory of that period of waiting for news from the hospital is of the hooting of the passing trains by which the leaden hours were punctuated. (metaphorical)

(c) Imagery and figures of speech

Words can be used to appeal to the reader's (or hearer's) sense of sight, or sound, or touch, or smell, or taste. By appealing to the senses in this way the writer (or speaker) makes his language more vivid. We describe this use of language as the use of *images* - or the use of *imagery*. (N.B. *Images* and *imagery* - despite their names - do *not* appeal *solely* to the sense of sight. An image may appeal to any one, or more, of the senses, as just described.)

Each of the following sentences contains an image:

1 The *rosy* clouds of early morning are held to be a warning of rain later in the day. (sight)

2 Away in the distance we heard the *stuttering* of light machine-gun fire. (sound)

3 The neat borders and *velvety* laws were the park-keeper's pride. (touch)

4 As a conversationalist she is handicapped by her habit of talking nonsense and *nicotine*. (smell)

5 We woke to the sound of the sea and we drew in great gulps of the *salty* morning. (taste)

As those examples show, an image is a figurative (or metaphorical) use of language.

Though images can, and often do, consist of a single word, they are frequently part of what are called 'figures of speech'. Even though you may not be asked to *identify* the precise figure of speech being used, questions on language often draw attention to their presence, because they play an important part in conveying shades of meaning – *nuances* of language.

The list that follows defines and illustrates each of the figures of speech that you are likely to encounter in English-language questions.

Alliteration   The repetition of *consonant* sounds. 'Two toads totally tired trying to trot to Tuttlebury.'

Assonance   The repetition of *vowel* sounds. 'The half-heard word stirred a response from the semi-conscious man.'

Euphemism   The expression of a harsh truth in language that is designed to soften its impact. 'He passed away (died) yesterday.'

Hyperbole   A deliberate and obvious exaggeration to achieve emphasis and force. 'I was so hot at the end of the walk that I drank gallons of lemonade.'

Litotes   Deliberate understatement to achieve emphasis. 'He averaged over 80 per cent in the three papers, so we may guess that he knows a bit of maths.'

Paradox   An apparent contradiction, expressing a truth. 'It was often said of the law of libel that the truer a statement was the more libellous it was.'

Metaphor   A comparison of one thing with another without the use of *like* or *as*. 'That foolish economic policy yielded a meagre harvest.'

Onomatopoeia   A deliberate echoing of the sound of the object or action being described by the sound of the words used to describe it. 'The deluge had made a morass of the track over which our squelching footsteps wearily fell hour after hour.'

Personification Non-human objects or abstractions are given human characteristics. 'The weeping skies depressed me and I was thankful when, at journey's end, hospitality smiled and my friends welcomed me.'

Simile The comparison of one thing with another, introduced by *like, as, such as.* 'He ran like a deer.' (N.B. Simile says that one thing is *like* another: metaphor says that one thing *is* another. In simile, the comparison is open, confessed, drawn attention to. In metaphor, the comparison is concealed. The two objects, qualities, actions are fused together.)

Used appropriately, and with originality, imagery and figures of speech add life and lend suggestive power to writing. Misused, they degenerate into stale, secondhand imitations of what the speaker or writer has heard or read. A deliberate attempt at 'fine writing' usually conveys a feeling of artificiality and affectation.

(d) Idioms and proverbial expressions

An idiom is a form of expression (or of grammatical usage) peculiar to a particular language and often having a meaning other than the one that it appears to have.

All languages have their own idioms. For example, in English we say that someone is 'as deaf as a post'; but the French expression (to convey the same sense) is 'sourd comme une pioche' - 'as deaf as a pickaxe'.

Similarly, in English we say, 'It's ten francs *a* bottle.' In French, the idiom is, 'C'est dix francs *la* bouteille.'

Mastery of any language demands a fluent use of idiom. That is why *literal* translation from one language into another often results in gibberish. We have to find equivalent idioms when translating.

There are hundreds of idioms in the English language. Here is a *selection* of the idiomatic expressions that include the word 'head': head and shoulders; heads I win, tails you lose; to have a head on one's shoulders; to lose one's head; to have one's head turned; to make neither head nor tail of it; to be off one's head; over head and ears; to come to a head; to head of; to hit the nail on the head; to keep one's head . . .

Obviously, nobody can sit down to learn all the idioms in the language by heart. You pick up the idioms as you learn to use the language. Idioms have arisen from a multitude of human activities and occupations, from the accumulated experience of generation after generation, until this very moment - and they continue to multiply.

The kind of examination question that involves a knowledge of idiom is illustrated by this test.

Test 19
Answers on page 171.
Rewrite the following sentences without using idiom. Do not change the sense.

1 I had not planned to take a holiday just then, but the offer was so good that I decided to make hay while the sun shone.

2 After a game lasting nearly three hours, Jones lowered his sail.

3 A man on the make is not to be trusted.

4 You cannot have much respect for a leader who passes the buck.

5 They were not enthusiastic about the scheme, but his forceful personality and eloquence roped them in eventually.

Proverbs and proverbial expressions are like idioms in that they are the distillation of centuries of general experience. Their sources are as varied as those of idioms. Books, the remembered sayings of famous people, the customs and traditions of particular groups of people, the tackle, conventions, and methods of a multitude of occupations – all provide us with familiar, everyday expressions: a stitch in time saves nine; Homer sometimes nods; it's hard to teach an old dog new tricks . . .

In using proverbial expressions we must be on our guard. Expressions that were fresh, vivid, and exciting when they were first used may well have been dulled with over-use. They have degenerated into clichés (see Section 5.7). They are then used by lazy thinkers and bad writers. One cannot say that this particular proverbial expression is 'good', whereas that is 'bad'. The judgement of whether or when to employ them is more complicated than that.

As a *general* guide, George Orwell's famous advice about the use of figures of speech may be applied to the use of proverbial expressions:

● Never use a metaphor, simile, or other figure of speech which you are used to seeing in print.

Orwell was encouraging writers and speakers to 'cut out all prefabricated phrases'. Excellent advice. However, proverbial expressions have been, and still are, much used, and comprehension demands that you know the meaning of a great many – even if you are (rightly) fastidious about using them yourself.

(e) Thinking and feeling
Words are used to make their readers/hearers think and/or feel. It is important to be clear about this fact, for in every situation in which we use language (and especially – as examination candidates – in composition, comprehension, and summary) both the meaning of what we write and our understanding of the meaning of others is profoundly influenced by this dual function of words.

A simple everyday example illustrates the point. Observe how the word *red* 'changes meaning' in these sentences:

(i) When you're in a hurry all the traffic lights are red.

(ii) Red is the colour seen at the least refracted end of the spectrum.

(iii) Don't mention the end-of-term party to him – it's like a red rag to a bull, just at present.

(iv) We thought the committee could carry that motion, but the AGM was packed with Reds and they threw it out.

It is not really the word itself that 'changes meaning' in those sentences. All the meanings that it has are 'built in' to the word. It is *used* in different ways to convey different meanings.

In some of the sentences it was employed so as to emphasise its 'reference'. In others, it was employed so as to emphasise its 'emotive meaning'.

To sum up:

- Words can be used as 'labels'. They then name and describe *things* and their attributes. This is language used factually and objectively. It is language used to convey 'referential' or 'denotative' meaning. The writer/speaker is saying to his reader/hearer, 'I am dealing with things as they are.'
- Words can be used to 'signal' feelings (emotional attitudes) which the writer/speaker wishes to communicate to his audience. This is language used subjectively. It is language used to convey 'emotive' or 'connotative' meaning. The writer/speaker is saying to his reader/hearer, 'I am concerned with the emotions that I feel about these things and I wish you to share in my feelings about them.'

In scientific writing and in the practical business-like writing of transactional prose the reference of words is (or should be) uppermost.

In creative writing (and especially in poetry) the emotive meaning of words is as important as their reference.

Reference (denotation) is not 'better' or 'worse' than emotive (connotative) meaning. Sense of *purpose* and sense of *audience* must be your guides to the appropriate use of words.

What – as writers/readers, speakers/hearers – we all have to be on the look out for is a dishonest use of language. If you study advertisements and political speeches or articles with a critical eye you will become aware of how often writers and speakers pretend that they are dealing with facts when they are, in reality, peddling emotions. They pretend that they want us to *think*, but they are using language to make us feel.

Compare these two newspaper reports. They exemplify the difference between the referential and the *pseudo-referential* use of words. Though set in the future they are representative of a contrast with which you are confronted every day.

The second passage is an example of the kind of linguistic dishonesty that is all-too-common. Your English-language studies should enable you to detect this kind of verbal con trick. In the examination you are (rightly) expected to be capable of discriminating between honest and dishonest uses of words.

THE DAILY EXAMINER
1 May 2000

Winding up the debate yesterday, the Minister for Space Programmes stated that although very great progress had been made in the design of reactor rockets the problems still to be overcome were considerable.

It was dangerous to prophesy on this subject, still in the experimental stage, and he wished the House to be cautious in accepting reports that had appeared in the more sensational organs of the Press. Such reports were based rather on the desire to excite their readers than on reliable information. He was referring in particular to recent statements, made in a paper with an immense circulation, to the effect that government timidity was responsible for the delay in launching the satellite planet. That was simply not true. The satellite planet had not been launched, because it was not ready for launching. Preliminary tests by the interstellar scientists responsible for design and development had show that certain modifications were essential. These were being made with all speed.

The Minister said that he was aware that the reports in the *Rocket* claimed authority from the opinions of Professor Octopod, but that, while he had the greatest respect for the work done by the professor in his youth on the muscular development of centipedes, he was by no means convinced of the learned gentleman's credentials to criticise research now being undertaken in the somewhat different field of interstellar travel.

However, Dr Atomson, the head of the government research team, had invited Professor Octopod to communicate his views to him in a memorandum, a mode of discussion that might prove more fruitful in this highly technical field than the columns of the *Rocket*.

As to the charge that the government was parsimonious with spaceship research, the Minister said that the fact that nearly six per cent of government spending was to be apportioned to it in the current financial year should be a sufficient answer.

THE ROCKET
1 May 2000

GOVERNMENT EVADES *ROCKET*'S CHARGES
VICIOUS ATTACK ON DISTINGUISHED SCIENTIST

A typically hestitant and evasive speech by the 'responsible' Minister showed an anxious House last night that the government is petrified by the *Rocket*'s refusal to drop its probe into the GREAT SPACESHIP SHAMBLES.

Unable to deny Octopod's scientific eminence, the Minister saw fit to sneer at his age before inviting him to help clear up the chaos that blundering bureaucrats have made in Britain's only Satplan Experiment. A curious way of appealing to him for the help that only he can give.

We know, however, that Professor Octopod will respond to his country's call, putting patriotism before personal pride.

In a feeble attempt to deny our charges of Treasury blight on vital research, a smoke-screen of economic jargon was let loose upon a bemused Commons.

Plain Men will demand Plain Facts in this scandal. We shall continue to press for the Plain Truth – whoever gets hurt.

THE STARS TODAY NOT TOMORROW! That is the *Rocket*'s rallying cry to Britain.

In this, as ever, we shall be the voice of THE PEOPLE.

5.7 HOW WORDS ARE MISUSED

A common and deliberate misuse of words has just been illustrated. The errors are, of course, not always deliberately committed. The following guidelines will help you to avoid traps into which we all fall from time to time.

- Choose plain words in preference to far-fetched words.
- Choose words drawn from the general vocabulary of the language in preference to words drawn from specialised vocabularies.
- Choose short expressions in preference to long ones – never use more than one word *where one will do*.

Failure to observe those three rules leads to pompous, turgid, windy writing and speaking.

(a) Plain words
As you have seen, the English language draws its vocabulary from many sources and has an abundance of synonyms. In Section 5.5 we used 'buy/

purchase' and 'live/reside' to illustrate that care must be used when making a choice of words. Unhappily, many people honestly believe that the bigger – the more 'important' word - is somehow 'better' than the shorter and more common word. Consequently, the plain, simple word often drops out of use and the once-far-fetched word replaces it. The 'big' word then loses the usefulness – the precise meaning – that it once had.

Your judgement of which word to select when you have a choice should be based on the context in which it is in which you are going to use it and the purpose for which you want it. Sense of audience and sense of occasion must guide you.

The young reporter on a local paper who writes: 'The bride's father has purchased a property to present to his daughter and her husband as their future residence' should be 'blue-pencilled' by his sub-editor. What he means is: 'The bride's father has bought a house which he has given to his daughter and her husband to live in.'

That does not mean to say that 'reside' and 'residence' have no useful part to play in our vocabularies. There are contexts in which they are 'right'. For example: 'Ranpoor House was the provincial governor's residence in the days of empire.'

The word 'house' would not be an appropriate synonym for 'residence' in that context. But the indiscriminating use of 'residence' instead of 'house' devalues the former word. It loses its special meaning and then ceases to be available for use in the appropriate context.

That simple example illustrates the principle on which you should base your choice between the plain, everyday word and the less familiar, more important-sounding word. Whenever you are about to use the latter ask yourself if it is right for the context in which you are going to use it. 'Do I want its special meaning here?' If the answer is 'yes', then go ahead and use it.

There is nothing 'wrong' with the polysyllabic Latin-derived words of the English language. It is just that they are often misused by people who think that their use lends importance and dignity to their writing.

You do not make yourself important by inflating your style – merely ridiculous.

(b) Jargon

The word 'jargon' comes from a French word meaning 'twittering'. A great deal of twittering can be heard in radio and television interviews and read in reports of the speeches and pronouncements of 'public men'. Take care that it cannot be read in your examination papers.

Jargon is a mode of speech or writing full of unfamiliar terms – words drawn from specialised vocabularies and then used in contexts in which they are not appropriate. Jargon words may come from the specialised vocabularies of science, or sociology, or economics, or the law - or any of the special fields of human knowledge and activity.

There is nothing wrong with the jargon word in its proper context. *There*, of course, it is *not* a jargon word! But in general use it loses its precise meaning and becomes merely trendy; and the jargon-user loses the respect - and often the attention - of his audience.

Examples of current jargon words are: parameters; paradigm; viable; scenario; orientated; escalate - just half a dozen selected from the vogue words of the day. Look each of them up in your dictionary. Then think about the contexts in which they can be used with precise meaning and in which they are, therefore, at home.

The two chief objections to the use of jargon words are: first, out of their appropriate context they are usually inaccurate; second, they give the audience an unfortunate impression of their user. He sounds phoney. He is trying to look tall by walking on tiptoe.

(c) Cliché

A cliché is a hackneyed expression, one that has been used so frequently that it has lost its force. Some clichés have lost their meaning. They are so wearisomely predictable that they succeed only in boring the reader. Cliché-users proclaim their dullness, their lack of originality.

Here is a brief selection of clichés, just to put you on guard against them. I cannot list more than a handful of the thousands in common use, but if you have a look at this list you will be better able to recognise a cliché when you see one. The words that could be used instead of the clichés are printed in brackets.

abject terror (panic); an ample sufficiency (plenty); at a loose end (with nothing to do); be that as it may (nevertheless); a bolt from the blue (an unexpected misfortune); in the cold light of reason (examined intelligently); common or garden (ordinary); cut to the quick (deeply hurt); done to a turn (perfectly cooked); eat out of someone's hand (be subservient to); to fall on deaf ears (to be heard but ignored); in fine feather (in good health and/or spirits); first and foremost (most notable, outstanding) . . .

It would be tedious to continue - just as it is tedious for your reader when you use clichés.

(d) Slang

Words and phrases that are used in colloquial speech are often unsuited to standard English. The *degree of formality* that is appropriate to the particular occasion is the measure of whether slang is permissible or not.

For instance, in a story composition it may be 'in character' for people to use slang in their dialogue. It may be effective for one character to tell another to 'pack it in'.

But if (in the practical writing exercise) you were writing a letter requesting an important person to speak to a school or college discussion society, you would not inform him that 'we usually pack it in at about 7.30'. You would inform him that the society's meetings are timed to end at 7.30.

I am sure that you would not be guilty of a gross use of slang such as that; but we all have to be careful to adjust our vocabulary (and our sentence constructions - see Chapter 6) to the occasion. Sense of purpose and sense of audience, again.

(e) Gobbledegook

Gobbledegook (defined in the *Concise Oxford* as: 'pompous official jargon') is found not only in the language used by bureaucrats, but in the language that you and I use when we strive to be important, to sound 'learned', to impress. It is then that we make 'turkey-cock noises' - for that is what 'gobbledegook' means.

Gobbledegook is the product of some of the linguistic sins described earlier. It arises from the following bad habits:

- using big words - to try to impress;
- using more words than are necessary - either to give extra 'dignity' to our utterances or to prevent our reader from understanding us quickly and clearly;
- using long-winded, roundabout expressions instead of direct ones - again to increase our importance;
- using passive and impersonal constructions instead of active and personal ones to give an air of authority to our pronouncements.

Here are some examples:

Big-word gobbledegook   My career with Phipps & Co was terminated in the September of that year, when I was translated to Hokums Limited at an enhanced remuneration. (. . . ended . . . moved . . . better pay . . .)

Redundant-word gobbledegook   The congestion on several of the motorways during the Bank Holiday was such that the traffic circulation flow was periodically frozen and brought to a standstill. (. . . at times . . . traffic . . . stopped . . .)

Roundabout gobbledegook   In so far as they can be projected, the adverse economic factors in the immediately foreseeable future are likely to be of the order presently pertaining. (The writer of that sentence can't get off his verbal roundabout. Not only is he using superfluous words, but his sentence construction is circular. The virtues of plain, direct statement are beyond him. Recast into English, this is what he is trying to say: It is unlikely that present adverse economic factors will soon change.')

Passive and impersonal gobbledegook It is desired to draw attention to the necessity that the regulations governing procedures established to ensure safety in the event of fire should be observed by all residents. (I/We/The manager remind(s) residents that they must obey the fire-drill regulations.)

As you can see from those examples and the comments on them the various kinds of word misuse often occur together. A writer who thinks that plain words will not serve his purpose is usually given to using too many words, roundabout – 'circumlocutory' – expressions, and unwieldy passive constructions.

(f) Danger signals
Whenever you are about to use one of the words and phrases in the following list, stop and think hard.

Far-fetched words (plain equivalents in brackets)

acquaint	(inform; tell)
advert	(refer to)
ameliorate	(make better; improve)
assist	(help)
blueprint	(plan)
ceiling	(limit)
eventuate	(happen; occur; result)
evince	(show; display)
in isolation	(by itself; on its own)
initiate	(begin; start)
locality	(place)
materialise	(come about; happen; occur)
a percentage of	(some)
state	(say)
visualise	(imagine; picture)

Inflated phrases

The use of these almost always brings out the worst in the writer or speaker. If you use any of the following you are usually heading for trouble.

in/with regard to	in the majority of
in the case of	in a position to
in relation to	will take steps to
in connection with	it should be noted that
as to	it is appreciated that
in respect of	a crisis situation

5.8 GOOD STYLE

(a) What is style?

The word 'style' is used in many different ways. We talk of a batsman's style; we say of a coat, a dress, or a car that 'it's got style'; we say that a man or a woman 'has style'; we talk of somebody's 'life-style'.

Above all, of course, we speak of a writer's style. It is not only the makers of literature and professional writers who have style. You, too, have style – good *or* bad!

The style in which you write is the *way* in which you carry out any piece of writing; and, as has been stressed, the way in which you do it must be suitable to your purpose in doing it and to the audience for whom it is intended.

Your style, then, is a reflection of your ability to choose appropriate means to achieve given ends. If the means you choose are appropriate you will have a good style.

One purpose is common to all the writing you do. Your purpose is to be understood. Therefore, the virtue common to all the writing you do is clarity.

Your style is revealed in your choice of words and in the order in which you arrange your words. Order and arrangement are discussed in Chapter 6.

(b) The elements of good style

Good style is, obviously, the antithesis of the faults discussed in Section 5.7. There you were encouraged to *avoid*:

- long windedness
- pompousness
- affectation
- slang, jargon, and cliché
- passive and impersonal constructions

Put positively, to achieve good style *you must try to*:

- be plain
- be direct
- use no more words than are necessary
- search your vocabulary for the *right* word
- use active verbs whenever you have a choice

Those are useful guides to good style, but they will come alive for you only as you deliberately use them in practice.

Reinforce the lessons of this chapter (and those of Chapter 6) by referring to the following books:

H. W. Fowler, *A Dictionary of Modern English Usage*

Sir Ernest Gowers, *Plain Words*

George Orwell, 'Politics and the English Language', *The Collected Essays, Journalism and Letters of George Orwell*, vol. 4

Eric Partridge, *The Concise Usage and Abusage*

5.9 VOCABULARY- TESTING

Try to work through all these tests in the course of your preparation for the examination. Many of them will send you to your dictionary for the answers. Some you should work through on your own. Others are suitable for team work - tackle them with a friend or as part of a small group, discussing them as you go along. Often a test serves its purpose best when it encourages you to look out for similar uses (or misuses) of words in the English of your daily life. It is only through your readiness to apply the lessons of this textbook to your experience of everyday English that you will get the help that I have tried to offer.

Test 20

Answers on page 172.

Fill the blank in each of the following with a word opposite in meaning to the italicised word.

1 He is a *profound* not a ... thinker.

2 Early on it seemed that he might be good at mathematics, for he tackled *simple* calculations successfully, but his limitations were revealed when he was faced with ... problems.

3 The old manager's methods were *rigid*, and all the employees hoped for a more ... approach when his successor arrived.

4 The examiners were surprised by his bad performance in the *compulsory* question in view of his good showing in the ... section of the paper.

5 The dealer was delighted to be offered a *genuine* antique after seeing so many ... in the course of a busy day.

Test 21

Answers on page 172.

Express in *one* word the meaning of each of the following.

1 causing, sufficient to cause, or designed to cause death

2 respect highly, confer dignity upon

3 preliminary discourse, sometimes in verse, introducing a play

4 put right, correct, amend, reform

5 immediately, without delay

Test 22
Discuss your answers when you have completed the test.
Use each of the following expressions in a sentence in such a way as to make its meaning clear.

1   to harp upon
2   to ride roughshod over
3   a square peg in a round hole
4   to look askance at
5   a *quid pro quo*

Test 23
The words paired up in this list are often confused. Use your dictionary and then write a sentence for each word, bringing out the different meanings.

1   practical/practicable
2   uninterested/disinterested
3   intelligent/intelligible
4   ingenious/ingenuous
5   cultured/cultivated

Test 24
Use your dictionary to discover the sense of the prefix in each of the following words.

1   cyclonic
2   expatriation
3   hilarious
4   hippopotamus
5   hexagon

Test 25
Without changing the sense, rewrite the following in plain English.

1   The Medical Officer of Health extended assurances to the subcommittee to the effect that the occurrence of one isolated case of typhoid was no necessary cause for undue alarm.

2   Speaking in this very same council chamber some twelve months ago I stressed emphatically, and with all the seriousness at my command, that the services of an outside expert engineering consultant should be called in to assist with advice the surveyor's department with the serious problem situation of subsidence in Chapel Street.

3   The Trustees have decided and come to the conclusion that residence within the boundaries of the borough for a minimum period of five years is going to be for the future an essential condition of qualifying to be con-

sidered for the award of grants that are within their disposal as Trustees.

4   The treasurer reported that there were serious financial considerations involved in respect of the prospect of completing the new housing estate by the target date that had been set and that a crisis situation could eventuate.

5   In the majority of instances householders who were tenants of the council informed the council's investigating officers in response to the questions put to them that they were satisfied with regard to the scheme for differential rents operative with respect to the rented properties within the council's jurisdiction.

CHAPTER 6

SENTENCE AND PARAGRAPH PATTERNS

Few of the examining boards ask specific questions on grammar, but the wording of examination questions - especially those set on passages for comprehension - often includes grammatical terms. Words such as *phrase, noun, subject, adverb* are used by the examiners to direct your attention to words in the passage on which they require you to comment. Unless you know the meaning of such terms you cannot be sure that you are carrying out the instructions.

An even better reason for understanding the outlines of English grammar is the fact that you can make words work better for you if you understand how *they* work in English sentences.

6.1 WHAT IS GRAMMAR?

The grammar of a language is a description of the way in which that language behaves. French grammar is a description of how the French language behaves, Russian grammar is a description of how the Russian language behaves, English grammar is a description of how the English language behaves - and so on.

Grammar is not a collection of hard-and-fast rules. It is more flexible (and, therefore, more useful) than that. Grammar gives an account of the way in which a language is used by those who use it well. A living language changes; and grammar takes note of changing linguistic practices.

Of course, it is possible to communicate in speech and in writing without a knowledge of grammar. We learn to use our language by listening, speaking, reading, and writing. The more practice we have in listening and in reading, the better we learn to speak and to write, provided that we listen and read attentively and apply the lessons of *good* models to our own use of language.

6.2 WHY BOTHER WITH GRAMMAR?

Because a knowledge of grammar is a handy tool. An understanding of grammar speeds up our language learning. Knowledge of grammar helps us to understand why some ways of using language are more efficient than others. It widens the range of linguistic resources available to a language learner. We all have to communicate with a great variety of people and in varied circumstances. A knowledge of grammar helps us to choose and use the forms of language best suited to each particular situation.

6.3 THE GROUNDWORK OF GRAMMAR

At this stage it is best for you to concentrate on three aspects of English grammar:

- the jobs words do - 'the parts of speech';
- changes in word forms according to the jobs they are doing - 'inflexions';
- words in 'clusters', as parts of sentences - 'syntax'.

Those three aspects of grammar affect our use of words. Together, they constitute grammatical 'usage'. We have to use words according to the practices of good usage.

A note on the plan of this chapter
Sections 6.4-6.8 provide the basic facts about English grammar. They explain all the terms that you are likely to need and they can be used for ready reference. Sections 6.9-6.12 discuss and illustrate practical applications of grammar. They are taken up with 'grammar in action' - usage - and especially with ways of building up effective sentences and paragraphs. You may prefer, then, at this point, to turn to Section 6.9 and work through to the end of the chapter, referring to Sections 6.4-6.8 whenever you find that the practical work involves grammatical terms and concepts with which you are not familiar.

6.4 THE PARTS OF SPEECH

(a) The same word can do different jobs
It is important to get this straight at once. A word is a particular part of speech *according to the work that it is doing*. For example:

1 We are expecting a guest tomorrow.
2 Is the guest room ready?

In sentence 1 *guest* is doing the work of a noun. In sentence 2 *guest* is doing the work of an adjective. The same word, but different jobs.

(b) The eight parts of speech

Noun: a word used to *name* something – e.g. table; Kate; honesty; team.

Pronoun: a word used to *stand for* (stand in place of) a noun – e.g. you; it; we; him; themselves.

Adjective: a word used to 'qualify' (describe) a noun – e.g. *new* table; *pretty* Kate; *firm* honesty; *beaten* team.

Verb: a word (or a cluster of words) used to denote actions, states or happenings – e.g. He *entered* politics. He *became* a candidate. He *was elected* with a large majority.

Adverb: a word used to 'modify' (tell us more about) verbs, adjectives, or other adverbs – e.g. He entered politics *reluctantly*. He soon became a *truly* popular candidate. He was elected *almost* immediately with a large majority.

Preposition: a word used to express a relationship between one thing and another – e.g. The letter *from* the tax inspector puzzled me. This is an excellent river to fish *in*. They were selling lettuces *at* 10p each.

Conjunction: a word used to connect one part of a sentence to another – e.g. I am fond of reading *but* I haven't been to the library lately. The customer paid by cheque *because* he hadn't enough cash. The lifeboat was launched *although* the sea was rough.

Interjection: a word (or words) 'thrown in', often to express a mood, and having no grammatical connection with or function in the rest of the sentence – e.g. *Well*, it was obvious to us all that he was tired. *Hello*! what's this? *Oh dear*, it's raining again.

It will help you to remember the eight parts of speech if you group them like this:

Family 1	*Family 2*	*Family 3*	*Odd man out*
nouns	verbs	prepositions	interjections
pronouns	adverbs	conjunctions	
adjectives			

Family 1 consists of words that name things, and words that describe the things that are named.

Family 2 consists of words that denote actions, states, and conditions of being, and words that describe (or modify) those actions, states, and conditions of being.

Family 3 consists of connective words that link words (or groups of words) to other words (or groups of words).

Thus to identify a word as a part of speech is to describe the work that it is doing in a sentence.

(c) Nouns
There are four kinds of nouns.

Common nouns name a member of or an item in a whole class of persons or things - e.g. man; farmer; dog; letter; figure. A common noun is the name common to all members of or items in the class named by the noun.

Proper nouns name an individual, a particular person, thing, or place - e.g. *Robert* is a hard-working man. Like his father before him, he is a farmer. Several generations of his family have farmed in *Staffordshire*. Proper nouns always have capital letters.

Abstract nouns name qualities or states of mind or of feeling - e.g. His *diligence* was rewarded by *wealth*, which his *benevolence* employed for the *welfare* of the community. Abstract nouns name non-physical things.

Collective nouns name groups or collections of persons or things - e.g. There are eleven players in a cricket *team*. Collective nouns name a number of items that are regarded as *a whole*: crew; group; fleet, etc.

Note Some writers list a fifth class of noun - the concrete (or material) noun. For example: water; rubber; nylon. In practice, however, these may be regarded as common nouns.

(d) Pronouns
There are five kinds of pronouns.

Personal pronouns stand for people - e.g. Let *me* have the ticket if *you* can't go. Personal pronouns may be nominative, accusative, possessive, or reflexive. For example: I (nominative) will let him (accusative) have the credit that is his (possessive) and claim none for myself (reflexive).

Demonstrative pronouns point to or at people or objects - e.g. I like *that*, but I suppose it's a lot dearer than *those*.

Relative pronouns relate to a previously used noun or noun equivalent (their 'antecedent') - e.g. The book *that* I am reading is due back at the library tomorrow. In that sentence *book* is the antecedent of *that*.

Interrogative pronouns introduce questions - e.g. *What* is that noise?

Pronouns of number or quantity - e.g. *All* are cheap, but *many* are of poor quality. Sorry, we've only a *few* left, but you can have *three* each.

Note The idiomatic use of the pronoun *it* in an indefinite sense - e.g. It is fine, so the match should start on time. Is it far to London?

(e) Adjectives
Many words function both as pronouns and as adjectives. You can distinguished between them by remembering that a pronoun stands *alone* in

place of a noun, whereas an adjective is used *with* a noun – e.g. Is that *his*? (pronoun) Yes, that's *his* pen. (adjective)

There are six classes of adjectives.

Descriptive adjectives describe the qualities of persons, things, etc. – e.g. a tall man; a black dress; quick intelligence.

Possessive adjectives indicate possession – e.g. Is *your* house for sale? Yes, and I'd like to bid for *yours* (pronoun) if I get a good price for *mine* (pronoun). See note above on the distinction between adjectives and pronouns.

Demonstrative adjectives, like demonstrative pronouns, 'point out' – e.g. I cannot think why you liked *that* film.

Relative adjectives introduce relative clauses – e.g. I'll give *what* time I can to it, but I'm very busy.

Interrogative adjectives introduce questions (direct or indirect) – e.g. *Which* way did he go? I asked him *what* decision he had reached.

Adjectives of number or quantity tell us how many or how much – e.g. *Few* voters showed *much* enthusiasm, and *ten* minutes sufficed to complete the ballot.

(f) Verbs

The verb is the most important word in the sentence. In fact, without a finite verb there cannot be a sentence. Later sections on structure and usage deal with verbal functions (and malfunctions). Here are the chief terms and definitions that you need at this stage:

Transitive, intransitive, auxiliary

Verbs used transitively   When the verb is transitive the action is performed to or on an *object* (in the grammatical sense of that term). For example: The electrician replaced the fuse.

Verbs used intransitively   When the verb is intransitive there is no object. The action refers / relates solely to the subject. For example: The electrician whistled.

Notes on transitive and intransitive   The word 'transitive' means 'passing across or through'. When a verb is used transitively the action passes across *from* the subject *to* the object *through* the verb. For example: The angry man kicked the door. Many verbs can be used either transitively or intransitively. For example: Solar Slipper is running at Epsom next week. (intransitive) BR is running twenty extra trains in the West Region. (transitive)

Verbs used as auxiliaries   An auxiliary verb 'helps' another verb to form one of its tenses, moods, or voices (see below, p. 133). For example: I *was* entranced by my first visit to ballet. The auxiliary verbs are: be; have; do;

may; shall; will. They all help to express tense, voice, and mood. For example: I shall travel tomorrow. The car was driven by my father. Has she telephoned yet?

Person and number

1 There are three persons: 1st; 2nd; 3rd.
2 There are two numbers: singular; plural.
Person and number play an important role in subject/verb agreement. See Chapter 7.

Voice

There are two voices: active; passive. The voice is the form of the verb that shows whether the person or thing denoted by the subject acts or is acted upon. For example: The electrician replaced the fuse. (active) The fuse was replaced by the electrician. (passive) In the first sentence the subject (the electrician) performs the action. In the second sentence the subject (the fuse) has the action done to it. When the passive voice is used it denotes that the subject undergoes or 'suffers' the action (*passive* means 'suffering').

Tense

'Tense' means *time*. The tense of a verb denotes the time of the action. There are three tenses: past; present; future. For example: I wrote (past); I write (present); I shall write (future). Tense also shows whether the action or state of being denoted by the verb is (or was, or will be) complete (*perfect*), or whether the action is (or was, or will be) incomplete (continuous or *imperfect*). For example: I was writing (past continuous, or past imperfect). I had written (past perfect).

Mood

Verbs have three moods: the indicative; the imperative; the subjunctive. The *indicative* is the mood used to make statements or to ask questions. For example: He caught his train. Did he catch his train? The *imperative* is the mood used in commands, requests, and entreaties. It expresses the desire of the speaker and the verb is always in the second person because the implied subject is 'you'. For example: Hand him the keys. Please close the door. Consider the penalties of failure. The *subjunctive*, though still in frequent use in many languages (e.g. French), is little used in modern English. It is, however, correct in utterances where supposition and/or condition must be implied. For example: If I were you I'd take their offer. (*Not* If I was you ...) As the following examples show, the subjunctive - rare though it is - plays an important part in expressing meaning: 1 If Johnson were fit, he'd be in the team. 2 If Johnson is fit he'll be in the team. In 1, where the subjunctive is used, the implication is that Johnson is not fit. In 2, where the indicative is used, the question of his fitness is left open.

The infinitive

This is the form of the verb containing the word 'to' For example: to walk; to think; to write. The verb has also a past infinitive: to have walked; to have thought; to have written. The infinitive is not finite! That sounds (and is) obvious, but it is worth saying. As soon as a verb has a *subject* it becomes *finite*, and it becomes finite because - with a subject - it is 'limited' by having person, number, and tense. The infinitive has no subject, so it has neither person, number, nor tense. For example: *infinitive* - to write; *finite form* - He is writing (3rd person singular, present continuous or imperfect).

The present participle

This is the *-ing* form of the verb: to wait/waiting. It functions as an adjective: Where is the waiting room? It is also used with the verb *to be* to form the continuous (or imperfect) tenses of verbs: I am waiting.

The past participle

This takes many different forms: beat/beaten; talk/talked; ring/rung; bind/bound; break/broken, etc. We learn these quite naturally as we learn the language. Young children often make mistakes with past participles. For example, they hear sing/sung, so it is quite understandable that they use bring/brung. Candidates for the English-language examination are not expected to make similar mistakes! The past participle acts as an adjective: The ice on the frozen stream cracked. It also combines with auxiliary verbs to form perfect tenses and the passive voice: He has spoken to the governors. His words were spoken quietly.

The gerund

Like the present participle, it is an *-ing* form of the verb *but* it functions as a noun, not as an adjective: *Fishing* is a popular pastime. The sick man's laboured *breathing* disturbed the other patients.

(g) Adverbs

An adverb modifies (adds to the meaning of) a verb, an adjective, or another adverb. *Modifying a verb*: Jet planes fly quickly. *Modifying an adjective*: Fuel for jets is very expensive. *Modifying another adverb*: They pay really well on the right routes.

An adverb can also be used to modify groups of words - phrases or clauses - within a sentence. For example: 1 We felt that we were nearly over the worst. 2 The government is regarded as a failure chiefly because it had promised so much. In 1 *nearly* modifies the phrase 'over the worst'. In 2 *chiefly* modifies the clause 'because it had promised so much'.

There are three kinds of adverbs: simple; interrogative; relative.

Simple adverbs tell us when, where, how, how much, or how often.

Time: They arrived early. *Place*: When the red light shows, stop here. *Manner*: He works slowly. *Quantity, Extent, or Degree*: We've nearly finished. I'm very tired. You've done enough. *Number*: Ring twice.

Interrogative adverbs are used in asking questions: When is your interview? Why are you so worried about it?

Relative adverbs connect two clauses. They *relate to* an 'antecedent' (a word or a group of words in another clause): We have visited the house where Shakespeare was born. I think early summer is the time when the countryside is at its best.

(h) Prepositions

Preposition means 'placed before'. A preposition is used with a following noun or pronoun to show relationship between persons or things or actions. For example: They must have entered through the window. Tell me about it. The mayor sent a letter to him and me.

A very important point is raised by that last example. A preposition 'governs' the noun or pronoun that follows it. That noun or pronoun must, therefore, be in the accusative (or objective) case. Be careful when a personal pronoun follows (is governed by) a preposition. Mistakes with case are common. The following are examples of *correct* usage: I sent a message to him. He sent a message to me. Don't broadcast this information, please – it's just between you and me for the present.

When the noun or noun equivalent is omitted, a word that was doing the work of a preposition does the work of an adverb: Meet me inside the public bar. (preposition) Meet me inside. (adverb)

(i) Conjunctions

Conjunctions are essentially 'structural' words. They link a word to another word, a phrase to another phrase, a clause to another clause. For example: Gin and tonic, please. (word to word) Are you going by car or by rail? (phrase to phrase) He left a lot of money, but his heirs soon spent it. (clause to clause) Each of those examples contained a *co-ordinating conjunction*. The words, phrases, and clauses linked by each conjunction were of equal importance, doing the same work as each other in their respective sentences.

Subordinating conjunctions link subordinate clauses to main clauses (see Section 6.8). For example: He was sacked because he was pilfering from the stores. I shan't buy it, although I like it. The successful general never attacks until he has an ample reserve.

(j) Interjections
Well, we needn't spend any more time on them! (see Section 6.4(b)).

6.5 INFLEXIONS

If you have studied French or German you know that they are 'highly inflected' languages. Adjectives 'agree with' nouns, gender is grammatically important, verbs are conjugated, nouns are declined, and so on - la belle fille / les beaux yeux; der, die, das; ich, mich, mir, etc., etc.

There are comparatively few inflexions in English. Here are some principal examples:

Personal pronouns: I, me, mine; you, yours; he, him, his; she, her, hers; we, us, ours; they, them, theirs.

Plurals of nouns: egg / eggs; gas / gases; baby / babies; donkey / donkeys; loaf / loaves; scarf / scarves *or* scarfs; potato / potatoes, *but* piano / pianos; man / men; mouse / mice, etc.

Verb forms: For example - to bring / bring / brings / bringing / brought; to do / do / does / did / doing / done.

Comparatives: sad / sadder / saddest; good / better / best; little / less / least; much / more / most; firmly / more firmly / most firmly.

We learn the inflexions of the language and how to use them by reading and listening to (and imitating) good writers and speakers. Good habits are catching - so are bad ones. Sitting down to learn a grammar book by heart is not the way to learn to use your native language. On the other hand, correctness matters. Chapter 7 directs attention to the mistakes that ignorance of inflexions causes. ('causes' *not* 'cause').

6.6 PHRASES AND SIMPLE SENTENCES

(a) Building with words
We use language so naturally that we rarely stop to think about the ways in which we build words into larger linguistic structures - into phrases, clauses, sentences, and paragraphs. While everything is going smoothly we neither wish nor feel the need to question what we are doing.

But we all get landed with problems from time to time and find ourselves sadly reflecting: 'I knew what I wanted to say, but I couldn't find the words' *or* 'I know I didn't make myself clear' *or* 'I didn't make the best use of the material I had' *or* 'I hope the examiner reads it in the way I meant it' *or* 'I know it wasn't a good way of putting it, but time was slipping by and I had to leave it as it was'.

By taking thought beforehand about the 'architecture' of the English language we can acquire a sense of language patterns that will stand us in good stead when we are writing under pressure and against the clock. The habit of building firm sentence structures and well-made paragraphs becomes ingrained.

We are now going to trace out some of the basic patterns available to us as writers, following this trunk route on our linguistic journey:

words as parts of phrases → phrases as parts of sentences → clauses as parts of sentences → sentences as parts of paragraphs → paragraphs as parts of whole texts.

By 'whole texts' we mean complete written passages of some length such as compositions, essays, letters, summaries, reports - any complete piece of writing consisting of more than one paragraph and having a beginning, a middle, and an end.

(b) Phrases as parts of sentences

1 at half-past eight   2 at him   3 on each front page   4 The newspapers arrived at half-past eight.   5 Their headlines shouted at him.   6 His photograph was on each front page.

The first three of those examples are phrases. The next three are sentences.

A *phrase* is a group of words that makes sense, but *not complete* sense on its own. It is not an *independent* utterance. It has to become part of - be 'built into' - a larger word structure.

A *sentence* is a group of words that makes complete sense on its own. It is an *independent* utterance.

Grammarians argue about the definition of a sentence, but for our present (and very practical) purposes the definition just given is satisfactory. It works.

Test 26

No answers are given. You must test your answers by referring to the definition of a sentence just given.

Build each of the following phrases into a sentence.

1 over the bridge
2 with considerable excitement
3 by the last day of the month
4 at the end of the film
5 after the election

Test 27
Which of the following are sentences and which are phrases?
  1 The delegate was shown to his place at the conference table.
  2 his brief-case stuffed full with papers
  3 The first hour or so passed in irrelevant and profitless discussion.
  4 mainly the restatement of their respective bargaining positions
  5 Real negotiations began later.

(c) Capital letter and full stop
Because a sentence is an independent utterance making complete sense on its own, it is necessary to mark it off from all the other sentences in a piece of writing. The first word of a sentence begins with a capital letter. A full stop is placed after the last word.

> I had no change. The ticket machine accepted only 10p pieces. I went across to a parked car. The driver was just getting out. He had only one 10p piece. He needed that for his own parking ticket. I was getting worried. My appointment at the dentist's was at 11 a.m. It was already five to.

Although that passage illustrates the correct use of capital letters and full stops to mark the beginning and the end of sentences, it is not a good piece of writing. It is jerky and childish. In later sections we explore ways of overcoming those faults. However, even as it stands, the passage is an improvement on this:

> I had no change the ticket machine accepted only 10p pieces I went over to a parked car the driver was just getting out he had only one . . .

(d) The finite verb
Important as the capital letter and the full stop are as 'sentence markers', a phrase cannot be transformed into a sentence merely by the addition of a capital letter and a full stop.

> The west wind the beeches at the bottom of the garden. Against his study window John Brown a faint pattering. He in annoyance. Rain a most unwelcome complication. In his planning he a possible interruption of the sunny weather.

That does not make sense. But slot the following verbs into place and the gibberish is turned into a sensible utterance consisting of five sentences in a meaningful sequence: was stirring – heard – exclaimed – would be – had not considered. Five finite verbs used in the right places build five sentences.

● The *key word* in the *sentence* is the *finite verb*.

(e) Subject and predicate

A verb is made finite by being given a subject. Every simple sentence can be divided into two parts:

1 The part that names the person or thing about which something is said. This part is called 'the subject'.

2 The part that says something about the person or thing named by the subject. This part is called 'the predicate'.

Subject	*Predicate*
John	ran across the road
The little boy	asked for a sweet
The aeroplane	dived steeply
Hens	lay eggs
The use of language	distinguishes human beings from other animals

Test 28

Answers on page 172.

Divide the following sentences into subject and predicate.

1 This is the twenty-eight test in this book.
2 It should not prove too difficult.
3 Every simple sentence contains two parts.
4 The two parts are the subject and the predicate.
5 The word 'predicate' comes from a Latin word meaning *to declare*.
6 The predicate declares something about the subject.
7 By containing a finite verb a group of words can form a sentence.
8 Despite appearances, there is only one finite verb in sentence seven.

(f) The simple sentence

A group of words making complete sense on its own is a sentence. A sentence containing *one* finite verb (and *only* one) is a *simple* sentence. Like sentence 7 in Test 28, this is a simple sentence:

A remarkable example of a replica of a famous Victorian dolls' house, complete with mid-nineteenth-century furniture and William Morris-design wallpapers, was exhibited at the trade fair.

There is one finite verb (*was exhibited*) in that sentence. It is, therefore, a simple sentence.

You could turn it about in several ways and still keep it as a simple sentence:

Exhibited at the trade fair was . . .
Complete with . . . a remarkable . . . was exhibited . . .

Experimenting with sentence order in that way provides useful practice in learning to control sentence structures.

6.7 DOUBLE AND MULTIPLE SENTENCES

As you saw earlier, a passage of writing consisting solely of a series of simple sentences sounds jerky. One way to avoid this fault is to combine two or more simple sentences into double or multiple sentences.

Simple sentences. I had no change. The ticket machine accepted only 10p pieces. I went across to a parked car.

Double sentence. I had no change *and* the ticket machine accepted only 10p pieces.

Multiple sentence. I had no change *and* the ticket machine accepted only 10p pieces *but* I went across to a parked car.

A *double* sentence has this structure: simple sentence + simple sentence.

A *multiple* sentence has this structure: simple sentence + simple sentence + simple sentence (+ any number of other simple sentences).

Double and multiple sentences are built up of simple sentences linked together by *co-ordinating conjunctions*.

6.8 CLAUSES AND COMPLEX SENTENCES

All the sentences that we have discussed so far have been *simple* sentences (in the grammatical sense of that term), for double and multiple sentences are in fact a series of linked simple sentences.

Here is a different kind of sentence:

I paid the boy who delivered the newspapers.

That is not a simple sentence, for it contains more than one finite verb. There are two finite verbs in the sentence: *paid* and *delivered*.

Nor is it a double sentence. In a double sentence each separate part (clause) can stand alone and make sense:

I had no change (*and*) the ticket machine accepted only 10p pieces.

But although 'I paid the boy' can stand alone and make complete sense, 'who delivered the newspapers' cannot.

So, although there are two finite verbs, one part of the sentence is different in 'status' from the other.

Each part is a *clause* – a group of words containing a finite verb and forming part of a sentence. But one of the clauses is an independent utterance and the other is not.

Main clause: I paid the boy.
Dependent (or subordinate) clause: who delivered the newspapers

A *main clause* is a group of words containing a finite verb, forming part of a sentence, and making the main statement.

A *dependent or subordinate* clause is a group of words containing a finite verb, forming part of a sentence, and *dependent* upon (*subordinate* to) the main statement.

Test 29
Answers on page 172.
Divided the following sentences into main clause and subordinate (or dependent) clause.

1 He was driving the car that I nearly bought.
2 This generator provides the electricity that drives the wheels.
3 Just as I reached the station the train pulled away.
4 Before the film ended the audience began to leave.
5 The whistle blew as he scored the winning goal.
6 I hope you understand main and subordinate clauses.
7 What I said at the meeting was reported in the papers the next day.
8 The answer to your question is that the economy of the country needs a boost.

A *complex* sentence contains a main clause (or more than one main clause) and one or more dependent or subordinate clauses.

A dependent or subordinate clause does the work of: an adjective, an adverb, or a noun.

Adjective clause: This is the time *when the ghost walks*.
Adverb clause: *Although he did not feel well*, he bowled fast.
Noun clause: I knew *that she was going to resign*.

As you can discover from any grammar book, there are several different kinds of adverb clauses (nine, as a matter of fact!), and there are five different ways in which a clause can do the work of a noun.

Examination requirements do not justify spending time on learning the detailed analysis needed to identify each separate kind of clause. The important thing for you to recognise is that each word (and each group of words) that you use in a sentence plays a part in the structure of that sentence as a whole.

The information about clauses given in this section will help you to develop your understanding of the 'architecture' of English sentences. In Sections 6.9 and 6.10 you will find help in planning the structure of your own sentences and in using a variety of sentence patterns.

6.9 SOME BASIC SENTENCE PATTERNS

The writer's need is to find the right kind of sentence pattern to fit the job in hand and to avoid monotony. Like his use of vocabulary, his use of sentence patterns should be guided by his sense of purpose and his sense of audience. His overriding aims should be to put his meaning across clearly and to hold his reader's interest.

(a) Simple sentences

Simple sentences fit the writer's purpose when he is describing rapid action, or making an uncomplicated statement. As an introduction, or a conclusion, or at a climactic point in an argument, the brevity and plainness of such a pattern may be invaluable.

But a prolonged series of simple sentences is jerky and monotonous. It sounds childish. It is inadequate to express thoughts of any complexity, especially where there are interconnected ideas and gradations of emphasis and/or importance.

(b) Double and multiple sentences

The combination of separate simple sentences into double and multiple sentences lessens the monotony, but the repetition of co-ordinating conjunctions soon tires the reader and draws his attention to the fact that the writer has a very limited range of sentence patterns at his command.

(c) Adjective and adverb modifiers

The inadequate resources of (a) and (b), above, can be supplemented by using accurately placed 'modifiers'. These, either single words or phrases, economise on words and tighten up constructions. The loose, sprawling *undirected* sequence of double and multiple sentences in series is transformed into tighter, more disciplined writing. Compare passage 1 with passage 2, below:

> 1 Exmoor was the scene of an experiment. The experiment was a remarkable one. It took place in the 19th century. John Knight ploughed up many acres. He was vigorous and inventive man. The land he ploughed was moorland. Up to that time it was barren. He also limed it. He used ox-ploughs. John Knight was followed by his son. He continued his father's work. He used steam ploughs. He got better results with these than with the ox-teams.
>
> 2 Exmoor was the scene of a remarkable experiment in the 19th century. John Knight, a vigorous and inventive man, ploughed up and limed many acres of barren moorland. John Knight's son continued his

father's work. The steam ploughs used by him were more efficient than his father's ox-teams.

(d) Complex structures

The improved patterns of passage 2, above, are based on the simple sentence. If you examine it you will find that it contains three simple sentences and one double sentence. The writer's purpose was narrative – he was describing a sequence of events – and those uncomplicated constructions were suited to his needs, but he wrote a taut passage by condensing and by slotting modifiers in. Note, for example, the adverb phrase of time.

When the writer needs to express ideas of any complexity, however, a more complex sentence pattern than that used successfully in passage 2 is essential. This is especially so when he must convey a main idea that is subject to qualification and/or extension. So, too, when he is dealing with several ideas, all of which are important, but some of which are of first importance.

The writer of the following discursive passage was arguing a point of view and advancing reasons to sustain his contentions. Only complex sentence patterns could serve those purposes.

I have already referred to scientific research, which is an integral part of the activities of our universities. However important may be the contributions made by full-time research institutes or from industry, the university must remain the centre of research activity in the country. There, after all, is the future research worker fashioned from undergraduate material. There is the fully fledged research worker most likely to retain a breadth of outlook as the result of regular teaching activities, often on subjects unrelated to his own research, and also through intercourse with those engaged in other disciplines. There, above all, he has the fullest opportunity to inspire others with his own vision. And if he does not do this, however brilliant he may be, he has only partially fulfilled his purpose.

Whatever lowers the standards of the universities as a whole, therefore, lowers the standards of scientific research, with all that this means for the country's future. All of us are most concerned at the ever-mounting costs of the National Health Service, but it is largely by raising health standards by the fruits of research that it is likely to be kept within bounds and made more efficient. The conquest of tuberculosis alone is estimated to have saved the country £60 million a year in treatment costs and in the productive capacity of young lives. Economies that affect our standard of medical research are, therefore, short-sighted, if only from a financial point of view.

In that passage the occasional employment of a simple sentence with conclusive effect is of particular interest.

6.10 THE GRAMMAR OF SENTENCE STRUCTURES

The traditional descriptions of English grammar outlined earlier in this chapter can be usefully supplemented by an outline of structural grammar, which is essentially a way of looking at sentence patterns. A sentence-based grammar (as contrasted to a word-based grammar) can often help a student to look at sentences with a sharper eye. This leads to an increase in the range of available sentence patterns and to an improvement of accuracy in sentence structures.

(i) The meaning of a sentence depends upon the *order* in which the words are arranged. For example, in the two sentences *The batsman struck the ball / The ball struck the batsman* we know by the order (and by the order alone) that 'batsman' is the *subject* in the first sentence and the *object* in the second. The word itself does not change, but we know from its position in the sentence (*in relation to* the position of the other words in the sentence) whether it is functioning as the subject or as the object. We know this because we know how the English language works. Our understanding depends upon the word order. It follows that, as writers, we must use words in their proper order if we are to make ourselves understood. Order is the first law of English.

(ii) Words often do their work in sentences, not as individual words, but as *clusters of words*. This is especially true of verbs. In the sentence *The wanted man was about to board a plane at Heathrow when he was arrested* the first verb is 'was about to board'. English makes constant use of *phrasal verbs* of that kind.

(iii) We get a clearer insight into sentence construction when we regard a sentence as being a structure built up from clusters of words than when we look at it as if it were made up of individual words added to each other. In the sentence just quoted, for example, the word clusters are: *The wanted man // was about to board // a plane // at Heathrow // when he was arrested.*
And here is a diagrammatic view of the same sentence:

The wanted man $\longrightarrow$ was about to board $\rightleftarrows$ a plane
at Heathrow
when he was arrested

Those two ways of dividing up the sentence are useful because they (i) show clearly each word cluster from which the sentence is built, and (ii) they show clearly the relationship that each cluster has with the others.

We can describe *at Heathrow* as an adverbial phrase of place modifying the verb *was about to board*. We can describe *when he was arrested* as an adverbial clause of time modifying the same verb.

But for practical writing purposes the important thing it to develop a sense of 'what goes with what'.

(iv) *The rule of proximity* states that those parts of a sentence that 'go with each other' to establish meaning *must be positioned as near to each other as possible*. If you break the rule of proximity you will write absurdities such as: 'Grandfather clocks are much sought after by collectors with brass faces and wrought-iron hands.' Observing the rule of proximity saves you from muddled sentences, ambiguity, verbosity, and downright rubbish.

Test 30
Answers on page 172.
Use the mark // to divide these sentences into their basic word clusters.
Example: The borough's newly appointed chief executive officer // was threatening to resign // within a month of his appointment.

1 Very few people are able to buy everything they want for their houses during the first year or so of their married life.

2 The result of the poll ought to have been declared by the presiding officer soon after midnight.

3 A red-faced customs official, apologising profusely for the mistake, returned the travellers' passports to them after a long delay at the airport.

6.11 TOPIC SENTENCES AND PARAGRAPH UNITY

Like sentences, paragraphs are built up from word clusters. In the case of paragraphs, each cluster is a sentence.

When we write a sentence we can either:

1 make the main statement early in the sentence;
2 hold it off until near the end.

For example:

1 The government hesitated to take steps to stimulate the economy because it believed that an increase in the money supply would accelerate inflation.

2 Because it believed that an increase in the money supply would accelerate inflation the government hesitated to take steps to stimulate the economy.

Sentence variety can be achieved by a writer who makes use of both those patterns: 'loose' sentences (main statement at the beginning); 'periodic' sentences (main statement at the end).

(a) The topic sentence

The sentence in a paragraph in which the main statement is made is called 'the topic sentence'. The topic sentence clearly announces the subject-matter of the paragraph. It is an essential 'signpost' for the reader.

(b) Paragraph unity

In a well-constructed paragraph there is *one* (and *only* one) main topic. That topic is firmly and clearly stated in the topic sentence. All the other sentences in the paragraph have a bearing on the theme announced in the topic sentence. Only by ensuring that the subject-matter of every sentence in the paragraph is connected with the subject stated in the topic sentence can *paragraph unity* be established and maintained. Paragraph unity is the foundation of clarity.

(c) The position of the topic sentence

At this stage you will be well advised to place the topic sentence at, or very near, the beginning of each paragraph. Later on, when paragraph unity 'comes naturally' to you – because you have deliberately worked at it – you may want to experiment.

At present your method should be: 1 Think hard about the paragraph topic. 2 Express it in a firmly built sentence. 3 Follow this with a sequence of sentences all of which bear on and develop the topic announced in the topic sentence.

(d) Good and bad paragraphs to study

Here are two well-made paragraphs. Notice the clear topic sentence with which each begins, and the disciplined way in which the writers connect all the other sentences with the topic sentence.

1 When a historian of the future deals with Britain in the 20th century he may well decide that the nation's biggest problem in that period was the preservation of freedoms won centuries earlier. Between 1600 and 1900 the laws of Britain slowly caught up with the growing conviction that the individual had rights against the State, and that it was the proper function of the latter to safeguard those rights. Yet, at the same time, social and economic pressures were developing that were to endanger the liberties of the individual. Those pressures were not fully manifest until the mid-20th century when, though sentiment was still in favour of the idea that the State was made for man, the revolutionary results of technological changes were threatening to reduce the status of the individual.

2 The idea that a conversation could usefully take place not in words but in mathematics is not as fantastic as it seems. Modern astronomers, using radio-telescopes, bounce their radio signals back off extra-terrestrial bodies. If, in one of the solar systems surrounding the millions of suns in the galaxy, intelligent life has evolved, the 'bounced-back' signals may stimulate 'live' transmissions. Since it is likely that such transmissions would be 'trying to talk', a common language would be needed if effective communication were to be established. Earth languages would be useless, but the operators of the stellar radios would undoubtedly understand mathematics. The first coherent messages might, then, take the form of an exchange of logarithms or decimal numbers or simultaneous equations.

A good writer follows the route that his topic sentence lays out for him. He does not turn back on his tracks. He does not turn aside into byways or go up blind alleys. He sticks to his main route until he reaches his appointed destination – the end of his paragraph.

Study the paragraph that now follows. Do you agree that in the first sentence in italic the writer turned into a byway, and that in the second sentence in italic he went up a blind alley?

It will help you to decide on your answers if, having read the paragraph carefully, you decide on a suitable title for it – the kind of title that you would give it if you were summarising its contents. When you have found a title you can test the relevance of each sentence to that title. Any break in paragraph unity will then show up.

The immense technical achievements of 19th-century Britain would have been impossible without the work of Henry Bessemer. *His system of producing steel was still in extensive use until a few years ago, though the open-hearth process invented by Sir William Siemens is now of greater importance.* Up to 1856 steel was an expensive product, imported from Sweden and costing about £50 a ton in the money of that day. Consequently, it could be used only for a very limited range of articles. *Wrought iron was used for engines, bridges, ships, machinery and railway tracks.* Bessemer's system whereby cheap pig-iron was converted into steel in huge retorts within half an hour – instead of the six days required by the older process – brought the cost down to £3 a ton. This meant that steel, which is stronger, more resilient and longer lasting than iron, was available for engines, bridges, ships, machinery, and railway tracks. Steel can also be machined more accurately than iron and is lighter. The development of the steam turbine and of the internal-combustion engine depended upon Bessemer's work.

6.12 SOME BASIC PARAGRAPH PATTERNS

These standard paragraph patterns provide useful guides when you are considering how best to develop a paragraph out of a topic sentence.

(a) Illustrations and examples

The paragraph is developed by supplying selected examples that illustrate the statement made in the topic sentence.

In Mrs Tompkins's kitchen on washday chaos reigned. Pulled out from under the draining-board, where it lurked for six days of the week, the washing-machine gurgled in its ration from the hot-water trap. Round it, a lake – fed by a leaky hose connection – rippled in the draught from the kitchen door. Half in and half out of the lake lay a jumble of dirty clothes, topped by a melancholy cat. At the kitchen table two rowdy children stuffed bread and jam into their mouths and into each other's hair. And Mrs Tompkins, maddened by the noise, darted wildly from table to sink, from sink to clothes, expending vast quantities of energy to very little effect.

(b) Enumeration

The paragraph is developed by listing items or ideas referred to in the topic sentence.

Thousands of words have been written about Rowlandson's career as a Test batsman, and study of the printed material suggests the chief factors that made him great. His temperament was equable. Neither elated nor depressed by the prospect of victory or defeat, he began every innings unruffled and played every ball strictly on its merits. His technique was as near perfect as is humanly possible, and while this enabled him to score freely it also fitted him for grim survival when bad wickets or great skill put the bowlers on top. Lastly, he was a superb judge of a run and, though hungry for boundaries, he never, at any stage of an innings, disdained quick singles that many other batsmen either could not or would not take.

(c) Cause and effect

The paragraph is developed by an exposition of the causes and effects referred to in the topic sentence.

Though outwardly cheerful and optimistic throughout a gruelling campaign, the defeated president confessed afterwards that he had anticipated his failure at the polls. As he had toured the country he had realised that his political advisers had underestimated both the ability and the popularity of his opponent. Further, though his own personal standing with the electorate remained high, some of his leading ministers had lost the confidence of the voters. Most damaging of all was the widespread view that the financial crisis demanded action sterner than he was considered likely to be willing to take.

(d) Comparisons and contrasts

The paragraph is built on a development of comparisons and/or contrasts stated in the topic sentence. A paragraph may, of course, concentrate on either comparison or contrast. The structure is the same in both cases.

The situation of Britain in 1588 and that of 1940 will bear detailed comparison. In both years a small maritime power faced a large, land-based enemy. The immediate and urgent need on each occasion was to stave off a threatened invasion. Only when that had been accomplished could means be looked for - by alliance, the gathering and equipping of land forces, and command of the sea - to launch an offensive against a distant foe.

As part of an essay that paragraph is nicely poised to lead in to its successor. The paragraph transition would be managed in some such way as this: 'But the comparison ends there. The two crisis years offer as much material for contrast as for comparison.'

(e) Definition

The paragraph defines a term (or terms) used in the topic sentence.

It is important to remember that the word 'tragedy' as a term of literary criticism or identification is - or should be - used more precisely than in its everyday applications. Newspaper headlines label as 'tragedy' every plane, train, or car crash that involves loss of life. In literature an event of that kind, though shocking, is not necessarily tragic. Tragedy, in its literary sense, is concerned with the downfall, defeat, or death of an individual or of a group of people whose overthrow, by reason of character or position, carries with it a significance for humanity as a whole. The audience (reader or watcher) is emotionally engaged in the fate of the tragic personages and feels their story to be meaningful for all men. *Macbeth* is not the tragedy of Duncan: it is the tragedy of Duncan's murderer.

A very conclusive end was provided for that paragraph by the apt illustration cited to support the definition. A satisfying 'rounding off'.

CHAPTER 7

RIGHT USAGE
AND WRONG USAGE

1 'Attention will be paid throughout to sentence construction . . .' 2 'Candidates will be rewarded for orderly and coherent presentation of material . . . and general correctness of spelling, punctuation, and grammar.' 3 'The examination will test the ability to write with facility, clarity, and accuracy . . . and to avoid mistakes of punctuation, grammar, and spelling.' 4 'The ability to construct and join sentences and paragraphs and to avoid mistakes of punctuation, grammar, and spelling . . . will be rewarded.'

Those quotations from four different syllabuses typify the requirements of the examiners in English Language, making clear how much importance is attached to correct usage, punctuation, and spelling.

This chapter draws attention to correct usage in those areas where mistakes are most commonly made and most marks are lost.

7.1 PROBLEMS OF AGREEMENT

(a) Subject and verb
The rule is that the verb must agree with its subject in person and in number. That is why it is *correct* to write: 'Candidates are reminded that examination results, especially in English and mathematics, are of interest to prospective employers.' It is *incorrect* to write: 'Candidates are reminded that the result of their examinations, especially in English and mathematics, are of interest to prospective employers.'

There are three main causes of error in subject/verb agreement. 1 Mistaking a singular subject for a plural, and vice versa. 2 Failing to identify the true subject and making the verb agree with an *apparent* subject instead. 3 Treating the subject as singular in one place and as plural in another.

(b) Singulars mistaken for plurals

These are all *singulars*: anyone; anybody; each; every; everybody; everyone.

Correct: All my journeys on that line *have* been uncomfortable.
Correct: Each of my journeys on that line *has* been uncomfortable.
Correct: Every man on that job *was* working as hard as *he* could.

Either and *neither* are *singulars*.
Correct: Either of these coats *fits* me, but I prefer the blue one.
Correct: Neither of his theories *holds* water.

Either... or/neither... nor when used in pairs can give trouble. When the two subjects are of the same number there is no problem.

Correct: Either Miss Jones or Miss Smith *is* going to accompany the children.
Correct: I believe that neither the politicians nor the electors *are* very clear about the issue.

When the two subjects are of different number the rule is that the verb agrees with the nearer of the two.

Correct: Neither the pupils nor their teacher *understands* the new time-table.

Kind; *sort*; *type* are *singulars*. If you want to use them as plurals, you must add an *s*.

Correct: I find *that* kind of book *pleases* older readers.
Correct: That type of question *is* being discontinued.
Correct: *Those* sorts of sweets *are* not selling well.

A pair of is a *singular*.

Correct: A pair of pliers *was* found in his locker.
Correct: Insulated pliers *are* esential for electricians.
Correct: A sharp pair of scissors *is* needed for that job.
Correct: Those scissors *were* stolen from my shop.

Some multiple subjects are singular. When the sense of the sentence subordinates one of the elements in the multiple subject to the other, then the subject is singular.

Correct: The chief inspector of accidents and his assistant *are* starting the investigation.

BUT *Correct*: The chief inspector of accidents with an assistant *is* starting the investigation.

Together with and *as well as* cause a similar problem.

Correct: The genuine article, together with a skilful copy, *was* on show.

Correct: The protestor, as well as his wife, *was* subjected to abuse and ridicule.

(c) Finding the true subject

The problem of 'attraction' crops up frequently. Plurals standing between the true subject and its verb 'attract' us into making the verb plural even when its true subject is singular.

Correct: A crate of bottles standing on the pavement *was* overturned.

Correct: A collection of his paintings *is* on show at the town hall.

Correct: That herd of cows *contains* some prizewinners.

In those examples the true subjects were all collective noun subjects. Greater difficulty arises when a non-collective singular noun subject is separated from its verb by plurals.

Correct: The wording of examination questions presupposes that candidates understand grammatical terms and *is*, in consequence, misunderstood by ill-prepared candidates.

(d) Collective nouns

These can be singulars *or* plurals, according to the sense of the sentence.

If you are thinking of the group named by the collective noun as a *whole* – as one thing – treat it as singular.

Correct: The team *has* been unchanged for half the season and *its* chances of winning the cup are excellent.

Correct: The government *has* decided that the compensation act must be amended.

If you are thinking of the separate individual items that make up the group named by the collective noun, treat it as a plural.

Correct: Occasional coughs, shuffling feet, one or two whispers showed that the audience *were* restless.

Correct: The plane touched down at 3 o'clock, and within a few minutes the team *were* through the customs and, after a tour that had lasted six weeks, *were* heading for *their* homes.

That last example illustrates the need for consistency. The singularity of plurality of the collective noun subject affects subsequent pronouns and possessive adjectives as well as the verb. All the parts of speech must be handled in the same way. Too often, you will hear or read news items in which consistency is flouted.

INCORRECT: The government has decided to give priority to their policy

for reducing inflation. (If *has* is correct it should be followed by *its*.)
INCORRECT: The jury have been unable to agree on its verdict. (If *have* is correct – and it is – it should be followed by *their*.)

7.2 PROBLEMS OF CASE

(a) Don't be afraid of 'me'!

The rule is quite clear and must not be broken: when the personal pronouns (1st person singular and plural) are in the nominative case (when they are the subject) *I* and *we* are correct. In all other cases *me* and *us* are correct.

> *Correct*: Do you really think that they are likely to give you and *me* an invitation?
> *Correct*: It has always been a problem for *us* idealists.
> *Correct*: The property was to be divided between my brother and *me*.
> *Correct*: The lawyer called in with the news and told my dad and *me* himself.

The last example, above, indicates the proper use of a reflexive pronoun.

The reflexive pronouns (myself; yourself; himself; herself; itself; ourselves; yourselves; themselves) are used to refer back to a noun or a pronoun that has already been used in the sentence.

> *Correct*: If you want something done properly, do it yourself.
> *Correct*: I was surprised that they fetched the shopping themselves.
> They usually get Mrs Jones to pick it up for them.

BUT INCORRECT: The members of the club presented my wife and myself with a silver teapot.

The writer of that sentence is afraid of *me*. He dodged it by substituting *myself*. I wonder whether he would have written: 'The members of the club presented myself with a silver teapot'?

(b) Relatives cause trouble

It is *grammatical* relatives that we are discussing! They often prove to be a trap, yet the grammatical rule is clear.

The relative pronoun takes its person and number from its antecedent and it 'passes them on' to the verb of which it is the subject.

> *Correct*: Some good critics believe her to be one of the finest novelists that *have* emerged in the last five years.

relative pronoun: that; *antecedent*: novelists; *verb*, have emerged . . .

Correct: In my judgement he is the best goalkeeper that *has* played for this club since the war.

relative pronoun: that, *antecedent*: goalkeeper; *verb*: has played . . .

When the writer has solved the person and number problem of the relative he can be confident about the case. The relative takes its person and number from its antecedent, but its case depends on its function in its own clause.

Correct: The officer at Branpoint was one of the many *who* retired from the service last year.

Correct: She was by far the best of the singers *whom* we auditioned yesterday.

Correct: Put Johnson down on the list of subscribers to *whom* we send the newsletter.

Correct: It is ironical, but I am quite sure that it was Peters, *whom* we sacked, *who* did such a splendid job for our rivals, Dart & Co.

Correct: He is the candidate *who*, I think, will win the election.

Correct: He is the candidate *whom* I think the best of a bad bunch.

7.3 DEFINING AND NON-DEFINING RELATIVE CLAUSES

(a) The relative pronouns
Standing for persons: who; whom; whose
Standing for things: which
Standing for persons or things: that

Though *that* can stand for either persons or things, we use *who* or *whom* when the antecedent carries a strong personal flavour. *Compare*: 'I am sure it was the man that I saw in the street' with 'I am sure it was Bill whom I saw in the street'. (We *never* use 'which' to stand for a person.)

There is an important distinction between *that* and *which*: Use *that* to introduce a defining clause and *which* to introduce a non-defining clause.

Compare

Correct: The road *that* links Stafford with Newport is the A518.

Correct: The A518, *which* carries a lot of traffic, links Stafford with Newport.

What is a defining clause? It is a clause that answers questions such as *Which one?* It gives us specific information about – it defines – its antecedent. 'The road *that* links Stafford with Newport . . .' (Which road? The road that links Stafford with Newport.)

What is a non-defining clause? It is a clause that provides a description of – but does not precisely identify – its antecedent.

N.B. The non-defining clause is *always* marked off from the rest of the sentence with commas.

There is a difference in meaning between these two sentences:

Students, who are entitled to free seats, should apply on the buff form.

Students who are entitled to free seats should apply on the buff form.

In the first sentence the relative clause is non-defining, and it is marked off with commas. The sentence tells us that *all* students are entitled to free seats and that they should apply on the buff form.

In the second sentence the relative clause is defining, and it is not marked off with commas. The sentence tell us that *some* students are entitled to free seats and that those who are should apply on the buff form.

All that sounds more complicated than it is.

Remember: use commas to mark off non-defining clauses; and use *which* to introduce them (when they relate to things).

Remember: do not use commas to mark off defining clauses; and use *that* to introduce them (when they relate to things).

7.4 MISPLACED MODIFIERS

Revise Sections 6.4 and 6.10 to remind yourself:

1 that modifiers are words (or groups of words) that modify the meaning of other words (or groups of words) in the same sentence;

2 that the rule of proximity is always to be obeyed;

3 that the meaning of an English sentence depends on order.

(a) Misplaced adverb modifiers

The adverbs: *almost*; *even*; *hardly*; *only*; *scarcely* are often misplaced. The writer must think hard when using them to make sure that he places them so that they modify the word or words that he means them to. The following sentences all make sense, but each means something different: 1 Only card-holders may pay by cheque. 2 Card-holders may only pay by cheque. 3 Card-holders may pay by cheque only.

Adverb phrases and clauses must be carefully placed. Crisp, clear writing depends on the writer's ability to get modifiers of this kind into their proper places. Obviously, you want to avoid absurdities such as: 'The policeman told the loiterers to move on in a stern voice.' No accurate writer would leave the adverb clause of time where it is in this sentence:

'The newly appointed headmistress realised that the school secretary when she got to grips with the problems was not willing to be of much help.'

(b) Misplaced adjective modifiers

These often result in such idiotic statements that most of us can avoid them, but you do see 'gems' like these in advertisements: 'Pre-1800 illustrated books sought by collector with leather bindings. 'Wanted urgently modern hi-fi equipment by dealer in working order.'

(c) Participial modifiers

Whether adverbial or adjectival in function, these give careless writers a lot of trouble. Study the following examples of *misuse* and decide how to put them right.

1 Travelling down the High Street the spire of St John's never fails to impress the visitor.

2 Ravaged by years and care the young man was shocked by his grandfather's altered face.

3 Gazing in the shop window the luxury goods were a temptation to the tramp.

4 When cooked the gas can be turned off.

5 Failing an improvement in essay writing he will not be a strong candidiate.

7.5 MISUSE OF PRONOUNS

(a) Ambiguous reference

Every pronoun must have a clear and readily identified antecedent. It may be possible to sort out the meaning of the following statement; but the writer makes it hard for his reader, by using pronouns ambiguously.

The chancellor's press secretary said that he would refuse to make a statement until the new measure was formally published but that he was confident that it would surprise financial circles when it appeared.

(b) No reference

It is always dangerous to make *it*, *this* or *that* refer to a preceding phrase, clause or sentence. In the following example *This* (at the beginning of the second sentence) defeats the reader's attempts to assign to it any precise antecedent in the preceding sentence.

Speaking in his constituency last night, the Home Secretary was eager to defend the government's record in liberalising the criminal laws, reminding his audience that he had set up a royal commission, that its report was expected soon, and that he would give urgent consideration to it, to the evidence submitted to it, and to the majority view as expressed in the vote. This must inevitably influence his judgement of this complicated issue and, he claimed, history's judgement of his record.

(c) Wrong reference
A frequent error, found in official correspondence and regulations. When found in an English Language examination script it is penalised!

A suitable candidate for this post will have good passes in English and in mathematics as well as passes in at least two other subjects at 'O' level. They will also have good shorthand and typing speeds.

7.6 MISMADE SENTENCES

(a) Sentence fragments
These occur when the full stop is used too soon and cuts off a piece of the sentence.

Examples of sentence fragments: 1 Each week the principal meets the student committee. Chiefly to discuss routine matters. 2 The pupil's progress was remarkable. Considering his previous carelessness and evident boredom. 3 The young policeman kept back the onlookers. While his more experienced colleague attended to the injured man.

(b) Run-together or fused sentences
Sentence fragments are caused by using a full stop too soon. Run-together or fused sentences are caused by using a full stop too late.
Examples of run-together or fused sentences: 1 My father bought me a train set when I was six later on he added accessories. 2 I must mow the lawn today there may not be another chance for weeks the weather is so bad. 3 Perhaps the best way of interpreting what politicians say is to believe nothing that is certainly my uncle's way.

7.7 CHOPPING AND CHANGING

Sudden and unnecessary shifts of voice, tense, mood, person and number are always clumsy and unpleasant. Often, they destroy the writer's meaning.
Improve these sentences: 1 As soon as the plumber found the leak its repair was begun by him. 2 The diary tells how Pepys finished his

bookshelves in April and in May he begins to arrange the books that he has bought. 3 Members of a club must obey either the rules or they will have to resign. 4 First, ease the retaining screws, so that the withdrawal of the cylinder may be performed. 5 Students were reminded of the importance of punctuality and that they should dress smartly for their interview.

Test 31
Answers on page 172.
Each of these sentences contains a common fault of usage. Correct each.

1 There are on this new estate, between the houses and the carefully placed blocks of flats, a remarkably successful example of imaginative planning in the open spaces, with lawns and trees.

2 This is one of the very best horses that has been bred in a North of England stable in the past ten years.

3 It is no trouble at all to any of my classmates and I to take it in turns to bring you books from the library.

4 Being tone-deaf the superb woodwind made no different impression on James than a badly played tin whistle would.

5 The kitchen needs painting badly so I suppose I shall have to do it myself.

6 If they will not assist with the filing us others will have to get on with it.

7 One is always at a disadvantage when you allow yourself to lose one's temper.

8 Being tired after a long journey he went to lay down before meeting the press.

9 Although Jackson was the heaviest, Peters packed a more powerful punch.

10 If, as may be the case, you find that raw meat upsets your dog boil it.

CHAPTER 8

PUNCTUATION

As you saw in Section 7.3, punctuation plays a vital part in communicating the writer's meaning. Its importance is made plain to examination candidates by the fact that they lose marks for bad punctuation. The trend today is towards lighter punctuation than was the practice only a few years ago: a trend that does nothing to lessen the writer's obligation to observe the accepted conventions.

This chapter lists the applications of all the punctuation marks that you must use. It also offers advice on those cases in which there is choice.

(a) The full stop   .   is used

1 To mark the end of a sentence, unless the sentence is a question or an exclamation.

2 To mark shortened forms of words. Its use as an abbreviation marker varies, some writers using a full stop to mark every shortened form. The following advice represents sound practice.

(i) Use a full stop to mark the shortened form of a word *unless* the shortened form ends with the same letter as the full word. *Examples*: Oct. - October   Dr - Doctor   Mr - Mister. Strictly speaking, Oct. is an abbreviation, but Dr is a contraction - the middle of the word has been left out: D(octo)r.

(ii) Abbreviations in very common use do not need full stops. *Examples*: BBC EEC.

(iii) Acronyms (names formed from the initial letters of the separate words making up the name) never have full stops. *Examples*: NATO UNESCO.

3 Omissions are marked by three full stops. These are called ellipsis marks. *Example*: What does the passage 'I declare . . . in the future' tell you about the speaker?

(b) The comma   ,   is used

1 To separate words, phrases or clauses used in a series. *Examples*: She bought flour, tea, milk, bread, and butter. She moved quickly through the barrier, round the shelves, past the checkout, and out of the shop. She walked down the street, found the bus stop, caught the first bus, and was back home in a few minutes.

Many writers do not use a comma before 'and' in a series. They would write: She bought flour, tea, milk, bread and butter. The argument in favour of a comma before 'and' is that it reflects the sense more accurately. *Compare*:

She bought flour, tea, milk, bread, and butter

with

Her breakfast consisted of coffee, cereal, bread and butter.

The example shows that the writer must *think* about his use of punctuation.

You will not be *wrong* if you use, or do not use, a comma before the *and* at the end of a series. Try to make your punctuation reflect the shade of meaning that you are conveying.

2 To mark off introductory words from the main body of the sentence. *Example*: In spite of this, progress has been rapid.

(i) In that example the reader would have wondered how to read the sentence if there had not been a comma after *this*. In such a case, a comma is necessary. *Further examples*: However, punctuation is lighter nowadays. Because of that, delay was inevitable.

(ii) When there is no initial doubt as to how the sentence should be read, the comma after the introductory word(s) may be omitted. *Examples*: In spite of this progress our profits are still too low. In such a case there is no need for a comma.

3 To mark off words in apposition. *Examples*: Napoleon, the Emperor of the French, threatened invasion. Our headmaster, Mr Smith, is retiring soon.

4 To mark off a person or persons addressed. *Examples*: In my view, gentlemen, we have got to economise. I ask you, chairman, for your ruling.

5 To mark off a parenthesis. *Examples*: Our latest model, mains- or battery-operated, is selling rapidly. The strategy, drawn up long before the emergency, worked very well at first.

6 To mark off a participial phrase. *Examples*: Turning over the pages, he realised what a masterpiece it was. Referring to our earlier correspondence, I find that your position has changed.

7 To mark off a non-defining relative clause. (Revise Section 7.3.) This is one of the most important uses of the comma. It is an outstanding example of the way in which the use of punctuation changes the sense of a sentence.

(i) A non-defining relative clause *must* be marked off from the rest of the sentence by a comma (or a pair of commas).

Examples: Commas, which are often optional, are frequently used puntuation marks. Rail concessions are available to old-age pensioners, who are often unaware of their entitlement. His final play, which was produced at the Aldwych on the day of his death, set the seal on his greatness.

If the comma – or commas – were removed from those sentences the meaning would be destroyed.

(ii) A defining relative clause must *not* be marked off from the rest of the sentence by a comma. (It is advisable to introduce a defining relative clause with *that* rather than with *which* when the relative refers to a thing – see Section 7.3.)

Examples: Commas that must never be omitted are those indicating a parenthesis. Cars that had front-wheel drive did not become common until after 1955. The report concentrates on the circumstances of early schooling that are most detrimental to the adolescent.

Continue your study of commas in defining and in non-defining clauses by sorting out the differences in meaning between the sentences that follow.

1 The anthropologist made an exhaustive study of the islanders who were cannibals.
2 The anthropologist made an exhaustive study of the islanders, who were cannibals.
3 People over sixty who are entitled to supplementary allowances should queue at Counter A.
4 People over sixty, who are entitled to supplementary allowances, should queue at Counter A.

(c) The semi-colon ; is used

1 To separate items in a list when the items themselves contain commas. *Example*: Extras obtainable for this model include: push-button radio, with or without cassette; electrically operated windows, separate control or master-switch; tinted glass; stainless-steel exhaust.

2 To separate clauses having a strong connection with each other that would be broken if they were divided into separate sentences. *Examples*: In an out-of-the-way place like this, old customs linger on; I have myself witnessed maypole dancing and Halloween rites. The immigrants had been led to believe that houses were easy to come by; however, six months of fruitless searching convinced them that this was not the case. Though,

no doubt, tempted to make political capital out of the issue, the Leader of the Opposition was fair in his comments; but, to everybody's surprise, the Prime Minister's supporters showed little eagerness to support their chief.

(d) The colon : is used

1 As an introducer. *Examples*: You will find that his actual words were: 'I do not wish to have an option clause included in the contract.' In the study the following lots will be sold: bookcases, manuscripts, typewriter, desk.

2 It is *occasionally* used to divide main clauses, but only when there is a dramatic and sharp contrast between the statements. *Example*: Man proposes: God disposes. You will probably come across this use of the colon in your reading. For your purposes at this stage it is better kept as an introducer.

(e) The question mark ? is used

After every *direct* question; and that *includes* commands and requests worded in the form of a question. *Examples*: Are you going to the match tomorrow? Will you send me a copy of next season's fixtures? *Do not* use a question mark after questions in reported (indirect) speech. *Correct*: They asked why our quotation was late.

(f) The exclamation mark ! is used

After interjections and exclamations. *Do not* overdo its use. Emphasis is better achieved by careful word-choice and sentence-patterns than by peppering your writing with exclamation marks.

(g) The apostrophe ' is used

1 To signal possession. *Examples*: man's cap; children's toys; ladies' dresses.

(i) To a singular noun add 's - James/James's cap.

(ii) To a plural noun *not* ending in s add 's - women/women's rights.

(iii) To a plural noun ending in s add only the apostrophe - boys/boys' shoes.

Notes

(i) Singular personal nouns ending in s sometimes cause trouble. Stick to this rule: when a singular personal noun ends in s make it possessive by adding 's - Keats/Keats's poems; Dickens/Dickens's novels; James/James's hat.

(ii) Multiple noun possessives. Add the apostrophe to the last noun – Barnum and Bailey/Barnum and Bailey's circus.

(iii) Compound noun possessives. Add the apostrophe to the last word – mother-in-law/mother-in-law's house.

(iv) *NEVER* use an apostrophe with possessive adjectives and possessive pronouns. They are already possessive. *For example*: Is that their car? Yes, it is theirs.

(v) *FINALLY*, remember that *it 's* means 'it is'. You must *not* use an apostrophe with the possessive pronoun or the possessive adjective.

Correct: The cat returned to its home.

2 To mark contractions. *Examples*: hasn't; didn't; two o'clock; the winter of '78/79.

(h) Inverted commas ' ' and " " are used
To indicate the actual words spoken or written. That is why they are often called *quotation marks. For example*: He said, 'Let me have your answer by tomorrow.'

Notes

1 A comma or a colon is placed after the 'saying' verb and before the quoted words.

2 Remember to close the quotation marks when the direct speech or quoted material ends.

3 Either single or double quotation marks may be used.

4 When there is quoted material within the direct speech it must be indicated. Study the following:
Either: 'Have you read Tennyson's "The Brook"?' he asked. *Or*: "Have you read Tennyson's 'The Brook'?" he asked.

5 Whichever convention you adopt, you *must* be consistent.

6 Study the following examples. They give the correct guidelines for all the uses of inverted commas that you are likely to need.

(i) The witness said, 'I cannot be certain, but I think it was just after midnight.'

(ii) 'I should have those brakes seen to,' said the mechanic.

(iii) 'It does surprise me', said the policeman, 'that you can be so very positive.'

(iv) 'Did the guide say that we should take the river road?' asked Tom.

(v) 'Can you be sure that my cue is "Have you seen him?"' asked the actor. (One question mark does the work of two.)

(i) Round brackets ( ) are used

To mark off a strong parenthesis. A pair of round brackets is used for this purpose when the writer feels that a stronger mark than a pair of commas is needed. *For example*: Caesar's ambition (so skilfully denied by Mark Antony) was feared by Brutus.

(j) Square brackets [ ] are used

To indicate that words enclosed within quoted matter are *not* part of the original material. *For example*: The crucial passage is: 'I do do not deny that it [the treasure] played some part in my plans.'

(k) The dash – is used

1 In pairs, as an alternative to the parenthetical use of round brackets.

2 To separate a 'summing-up statement' from the items that have preceded it. *For example*: The layout, the circuit, the components, the materials – all add up to an entirely new concept for such a transmitter.

(l) The hyphen - is used

To link together the elements of compound words. *For example*: mother-in-law.

Many words that begin as hyphened words lose the hyphen as they are absorbed into common use. *For example*: lookout; seaplane.

However, the hyphen plays a vital part in some words. Study the following:

1 Have you re-covered/recovered your umbrella?

2 I hear that all the players have re-signed/resigned.

CHAPTER 9

SPELLING

Marks are deducted for bad spelling, so you must do all you can to raise your performance. The main source of help is your own determination to become a good speller, but here are some useful tips to make it easier for you.

First, some general advice:

1 Read a lot. Then, when you want to use words that you have read, attempt to *visualise* them. Try to recall what they looked like when you saw them in print.

2 *Think* hard about spelling. You know which words you find difficult to spell. Pinpoint where you go wrong in the words that you misspell. Concentrate on your errors in a methodical way. You will soon find that you are making fewer mistakes.

(a) Syllablising
Revise 5.4. Good examples of the help that the habit of syllablising gives are: vet/er/in/ary; tem/per/at/ure; Feb/ru/ary.

(b) Prefixes and suffixes
Revise Section 5.4. If you notice word formation you will not go wrong with for example: disappoint (dis+appoint); dissatisfaction (dis+satisfaction); innocent (in+nocent - *nocere*, Latin = 'to hurt'); unnatural (un+natural).

Double consonants at the 'joint' of some words will be far less troublesome if you remember the effect of 'assimilation'. See Section 5.4 - *il*legal; co*ll*apse; a*tt*ract; a*cc*o*mm*odation.

(c) The spelling rules
Although English spelling is not very 'law-abiding', there are some rules that you should know.

Rule 1: *i* before *e*, when the sound is *ee*, EXCEPT after *c*.

For example: piece; grief; achieve; siege; wield; relieve; shield; priest; mischief.

BUT: receipt; receive; receiver; deceit; deceive; deceiver; conceive; conceit; conceiver.

AND, when the sound is NOT *ee*: deign; reign; feign; rein; vein; skein; neigh; weigh; weight; veil; feint; eight.

AND some more *ei* words with other sounds: heir; their; sovereign; foreign; height; sleight; forfeit; leisure.

Rule 2: When a word ends with *e* and you add to it:
DROP the *e* when the addition begins with a vowel.
For example: wake/waking; hate/hating.
KEEP the *e* when the additon begins with a consonant.

For example: wake/wakeful; hate/hateful.
EXCEPTIONS: awe/awful; true/truly; due/duly; paste/pastry; argue/argument.

Rule 3: When a word ends with *ce* or *ge* and you add to it keep the *e* when the addition begins with *a* or *o*.

For example: peace/peaceable; outrage/outrageous.

Rule 4: When a *stressed* syllable with a *short* vowel precedes a consonant, double the consonant when adding to the word.

For example: mat/matting/matted; rat/ratting/ratted; begin/beginning; dim/dimming/dimmed; transmit/transmitting/transmitted; propel/pro-pelling/propelled/propellor.

Rule 5: When an *unstressed* syllable with a *short* vowel precedes a conson-ant *do not* double the consonant when adding to the word.

For example: profit/profiting/profited; limit/limiting/limited.

Rule 6: When the vowel before the consonant is *long* double the consonant when adding to the word.

For example: refer/referring/referred; prefer/preferring/preferred.

Rule 7: Singular words ending in *vowel+y* (e.g. donkey) form their plurals by adding *s*.

For example: donkey/donkeys: chimney/chimneys; valley/valleys; alloy/alloys.

Rule 8: Singular words ending in *consonant+y* (e.g. baby) form their plurals by changing the *y* into *i* and adding *es*.

For example: baby/babies; lady/ladies; territory/territories; parody/parodies.

Rule 9: Most words ending in *our* drop the *u* when the suffix *-ous* is added.

For example: humour/humorous; labour/laborious; valour/valorous.

Rule 10: Most words ending in *double l* drop one *l* when combined with other words.

For example: cup+full = cupful; skill+full = skilful; well+come = welcome; all+ways = always; all+though = although; all+together = altogether; all+so = also; all+ready = already; (BUT all right - *always* the two separate words); full+fill = fulfil; cheer+full = cheerful.

There are other spelling 'rules', but they have so many exceptions that I do not think they are very useful.

The ten rules just given are helpful. At least, if you obey them you will be right far more often than you will be wrong.

(d) Groups of words

We all use our own mnemonics to help us to avoid our own habitual spelling mistakes. Many a pupil has mastered 'Mississippi' by chanting the word to himself rhythmically: 'M - i - *double s* - i - *double s* - i - *double p* - i'.

Grouping words according to their similarities of spelling is a useful way of tackling your own 'pet' mistakes. Here are some suggestions. Add words to each group as you come across them.

Group 1: *verbs in '-ise' and nouns in '-ice'*
verbs: advise; devise; license; practise; prophesy.
nouns: advice; device; licence; practice; prophecy.

Group 2: *words ending in '-ence'*
convenience; difference; experience; pestilence.

Group 3: *words ending in '-ible'*
accessible; admissible; audible; contemptible; convertible; eligible; feasible; flexible; forcible; imperceptible; incredible; indefensible; inedible; intelligible; invincible; invisible; irresistible; legible; permissible; plausible; reprehensible; responsible; sensible; susceptible; tangible; terrible.

Group 4: *words ending in '-ness'*
cleanness; greenness; keenness; meanness; plainness; sternness; suddenness.

Group 5: *words ending in '-age'; '-ar'; and '-or'*
average; courage; damage; sausage; village; calendar; circular; grammar; particular; author; councillor; radiator; surveyor; mentor.

Group 6: *plurals in '-oes'*
cargoes; mosquitoes; potatoes; tomatoes; volcanoes.

Group 7: *plurals in '-os'*
commandos; dynamos; photos; radios; solos.

Group 9: *common confusables*
accept/except; access/excess; affect/effect; allusion/illusion; altar/alter;
ascent/assent; capital/capitol; choose/chose; clothes/cloths; coarse/course;
complement/compliment; conscience/conscious; council/counsel; descent/
decent; desert/dessert; dairy/diary; dual/duel; dyeing/dying; formally/
formerly; later/latter; lead/led; loose/lose; peace/piece; personal/personnel;
principal/principle; quiet/quite; respectfully/respectively; stationary/
stationery; their/there; to/too; weather/whether.

ANSWERS TO TESTS

Test 1, page 3
1 P.   2 I.   3 P.   4 I.   5 I.

Test 2, page 3
1 Key words: *story*; *A Narrow Escape*
2 Notes on key words: *story* – examiner has specified a particular kind of imaginative composition – what are the characteristics of a story? – plot – characters – setting – action – dialogue – composition must contain some or all of those characteristics to be an acceptable answer to the question. 'A Narrow Escape' – title is specified – story has got to be of a kind that lives up to title – probably an exciting adventure, ending in 'a near miss' – could it be humorous? – could it be based on real life? – have I got the material for this in my own experience? – must I base my story on narrow escapes that I've read about or seen on television? – how *can* I be original?
3 Key words: *description*; *how to mend*; *puncture*; *bicycle tyre*; *benefit of reader who has never performed the operation.*
4 The key words in the second sentence in the instructions. I must put myself in somebody else's place. What would such a person find difficult to understand? Names of things used? How to use them? Order (sequence) in which various stages of operation are carried out?

Test 3, page 8
1 Narrative.   2 Descriptive.   3 Descriptive, but could contain narrative and dramatic elements.   4 Discursive.   5 Discursive; but could be descriptive with narrative and/or discursive elements.   6 Conversational.
7 Impressionistic.   8 Impressionistic.

Test 8, page 23
1 No answer – for discussion.
2 The writer chose to take the aspects that he selected in *ascending* order

of importance, leaving the most important to the end and thus bringing his discussion to a climax.

3 The loose end: 'making cars too expensive for all but the rich'. The writer sees a continuing problem, but he does nothing to suggest a solution. His reader is left with these unanswered questions: 'Are the rich to be allowed to have cars when other people are not?' 'What effect would that have on the advantages that the writer predicts from the ending of private motoring?' 'Would the provision of public transport suffer?' 'Would this be a just state of affairs?' All those doubts spring from just one loose end. They seem to constitute a serious weakening of an otherwise thorough treatment of a subject that demands (and, on the whole, has received) closely reasoned argument.

4 Suggested summary: 'Although the motor-car can bring benefits to individuals its serious effects on public transport and the environment outweigh its advantages. However, the growing expense of private motoring and the dwindling of available fuel will put an end to it and cure the ill effects for which the car has been responsible.'

Test 9, page 34
The inclusion of that material enabled him to round off his report by indicating the enthusiasm with which the keynote address was received.

Test 10, page 38
21st June, 1981.   Cluttered. Are the following really necessary? - *st* - comma after *June* - full stop at end.
June 21st, 1981.   Too many punctuation marks. Date is always clearer if day date is separated from year.
21/6/81   Clear, but 'cold' and offputting, especially when used in an informal letter.
21.6.81   Too many 'points' and not instantly clear.
21 June 1981   The best form in every way: logical progression from day to month to year.

Test 11, page 39
1 Comma omitted at end of salutation.
2 First line of letter in wrong place.
3 Comma omitted at end of salutation. First line of body of letter not indented.
4 *Dear* should begin with capital *D*. Comma omitted at end of salutation.

Test 12, page 40
1 Capital *S*.
2 Full stop after signature. Spelling mistake.

3 Comma omitted after *sincerely*.
4 Capital *F*. Full stop inserted after signature.
5 Comma omitted after *faithfully*.
6 Capital *E*. Comma omitted after *ever*.

Test 15, page 93
Gist of passage: Not until slow-motion pictures were invented, late in the 19th century, could artists represent galloping horses realistically.
Main points.
1 Legs of galloping horse move too quickly for human eyesight to identify separate movements.
2 Before invention of slow-motion films artists used one of two conventions:

 either (a) with front legs in air;
 or (b) with front legs stretched forwards and rear legs stretched backwards.

3 (a) Horses do stand on hind legs, but not when running;
 (b) Legs stretched looked speedy, but obviously untrue to nature.
4 Slow-motion films enabled artists to study horses' leg movements and to represent them accurately.
Note. The original passage contains 220 words. The examiner's word limit for the summary will dictate how much of the detail in the plan you will use. A 50-word limit is likely. That would entail telescoping points 2 and 3 of the plan.

Test 16, page 96
The chief opposition spokesman for education said that he had listened to the minister's speech with care but that he had found nothing new or constructive in its proposals. Indeed, he regarded that speech as a flagrant betrayal of the election promises made by the minister's party. Far from spending more on education, the minister proposed to hold expenditure at the level of the current year. In a time of rising prices that was tantamount to reducing the money spent on education, and he accused the minister of weakening the service that it was his duty to strengthen.

Test 18, page 103
largely is the first entry on page 639; *last* is the last entry on the same page

Test 19, page 116
1 ... I decided to take advantage of the opportunity
2 ... Jones admitted defeat
3 ... looking after his own advantage
4 ... evades responsibility by passing it to someone else
5 ... persuaded them to take part in the scheme

Test 20, page 125
1 superficial   2 complex   3 flexible   4 optional   5 fakes

Test 21, page 125
1 fatal   2 honour   3 prologue   4 ameliorate   5 forthwith

Test 28, page 139

Subject	Predicate
1 This	is the twenty-eighth test in this book
2 It	should not prove too difficult
3 Every sentence	contains two parts
4 The two parts	are the subject and the predicate
5 The word 'predicate'	comes from a Latin word meaning *to declare*
6 The predicate	declares something about the subject
7 a group of words	By containing a finite verb can form a sentence
8 only one finite verb	Despite appearances is there in sentence seven

Test 29, page 141

Main clause	Subordinate clause
1 He was driving the car	that I nearly bought
2 This generator provides the electricity	that drives the wheels
3 the train pulled away	Just as I reached the station
4 the audience began to leave	Before the film ended
5 The whistle blew	as he scored the winning goal
6 I hope	you understand main and subordinate clauses
7 What I said at the meeting	was reported in the papers next day
8 The answer to your question is	that the economy of the country needs a boost

Test 30, page 145
1 ...people // ... buy // ... houses // ... life.   2 ... poll // ... declared // ... officer // ... midnight.   3 ... mistake // ... returned // ... them // ... airport.

Test 31, page 158
1 is.   2 have.   3 me.   4 move the participial phrase.   5 position of badly.   6 we.   7 one - you - one's!   8 lie.   9 heavier.   10 poor dog!